|| ||| ||| ||| ||| | ||| ||| || ||| ||| ||| |||

W9-AVG-292

DATE DUE

5 MAY 1971 D D

MAY 15 '89 ENDS   MAY 12 '88 RED

OCT 11 1990   **BIRD**   SEP 2 0 1990

BIRD

MAY 15 1991   *BIRD*

Climbing Blind

COLETTE RICHARD

Climbing Blind

TRANSLATED BY NORMAN DALE

With a Foreword by Maurice Herzog
and a Preface by Norbert Casteret

NEW YORK
E. P. DUTTON & CO., INC.
1967

First published in the U.S.A. 1967 by E. P. Dutton & Co.,
Inc. / English translation copyright © 1966 by Hodder
and Stoughton Ltd., London, and E. P. Dutton & Co., Inc.,
New York / All rights reserved. Printed in the U.S.A. /
No part of this book may be reproduced in any form without
permission in writing from the publisher, except by a reviewer
who wishes to quote brief passages in connection with a
review written for inclusion in a magazine, newspaper or
broadcast. / Published simultaneously in Canada by
Clarke, Irwin & Company Limited, Toronto and Vancouver
/ Library of Congress Catalog Card Number: 67-10064 /
FIRST EDITION

Published in France 1965 under the title *Des Cimes Aux
Cavernes* / Copyright © 1965 by Editions Salvator,
Mulhouse

G
512
R48
A33
1967

For my dear parents.
To all my climbing and pot-holing team-mates.
To all those who, wearied by the struggle, may
one day lack the will to go on.

236672

Foreword

THIS is a fine book and a great book. It tells of a girl who one day resolved to become a mountaineer and a cave-explorer. She let nothing stand in her way. She explored the principal caves in the Pyrenees. She climbed in the most beautiful, but not the least dangerous, region of the Alps, the Massif de Chamonix. She "did" the Mont Tondu, the Col du Geant, the Infranchissable (11,000 feet) and the Mont Blanc du Tacul (over 13,000 feet)—difficult climbs even for experienced mountaineers. But Colette Richard came late to mountaineering; and she had another handicap—she is blind.

She tells her story with a perfect simplicity. We share her fears, her hopes and her delight. I have no hesitation in saying that the world today has need of this sort of testimony. In an age when phoney exploits flourish, of questionable performances and faked records, Colette Richard has restored its true meaning to that marvellous word, Adventure.

She also shows us that no difficulties are insurmountable, that it is a matter of challenging the world, challenging ourselves and conquering our own weaknesses. How can one refrain from quoting the old French saying in connection with her: " 'impossible' is not French"?

I hope all young people will read this book. They will derive from it a rare lesson in courage and an inspiration not easily forgotten.

Maurice Herzog

Preface

IT has happened to me often enough that someone who has written a book—a friend, a fellow speleologist or even someone unknown to me—has asked me to write a Preface. Here the case is reversed. It was I who asked the author, despite her youth, if I might write an introduction to her book, and I am honoured to have been permitted to do so.

Colette Richard's story, that of a blind person who is both mountaineer and cave-explorer, is surprising and moving. It is also edifying and inspiring; and above all it offers us a lesson and an admirable example of determination, love and faith.

Inevitably there exists between author and reader the gulf which separates the seeing from the sightless, and which makes it hard for us to understand how a blind girl could "contemplate" mountains and describe subterranean sights and scenes as though she actually saw them.

We have to tread warily in writing about the blind, or we are likely to fall into the errors common to all persons possessed of sight. Georges Duhamel has written:

"The blind confront the seeing with a number of painful problems to which popular belief, superstition and literature have supplied answers, often in good faith and prompted by sincere sympathy, which lack any basis of experience and, in a word, intelligence. There are many sensitive and good men who ask themselves every day, and almost every night, what their life would be like if they found themselves deprived of one of the senses whereby they gain their knowledge of the universe."

Colette Richard here supplies answers to our questions, our objections and our puzzlement. She does so with a candour, simplicity and good humour that are unsurpassed—I had nearly written "unprecedented".

But let us make no mistake about it, she has faced almost unbelievable difficulties and dangers.

I can recall three instances when, having the reflexes and vision of a normally-sighted person, I was for a short time deprived of the use of my eyes. The first two occasions were in the course of solitary exploration underground when my lamp failed me. To be suddenly plunged into that absolute and eternal darkness was among the most terrifying experiences I have known as a cave-explorer.

The third time was quite different. It was a deliberate experiment, carried out not underground but in the mountains.

I was traversing a steep slope of hard-frozen snow, and thinking suddenly of Colette Richard and wanting to get some idea of what it was like for her, I resolved to make twenty steps with my eyes closed. I had to cut the steps with my ice-axe, feeling my way, and it cost me a great effort to do ten, struggling all the time against the temptation to open my eyes. I carried on, but in my haste to finish and be rid of my handicap, temporary though it was, I fell at the thirteenth step and went into a full-length slide. Instantly, and instinctively, I braked vigorously with my ice-axe, at the same time opening my eyes. Having thus proved to myself how little capable I was of operating without the use of sight, I did not repeat the experiment.

That is a trifling incident, but it affords some indication of the immense courage and resolution required in a girl who, from love of mountains and caves, did not hesitate to undergo extreme fatigue and to run the especial risks that must obviously confront a blind person attempting these activities. It is true that she is sustained by a deep religious sense which is as manifest in her conversation as it is in her writing. God is present in her book, a constantly perceptible Presence, and it is this faith, which is said to move mountains, that has enabled her both to climb them and to penetrate to their depths.

In writing Colette Richard often uses the words "see" and "look", but this is simply for the sake of convenience. The fact is that she can see nothing. As she herself tells us, such power of sight as she possesses is only enough to enable her to distinguish between light and darkness. Nevertheless, having accomplished the almost unbelievable feat of climbing and "contemplating" lofty peaks, she set about realising a still older ambition, that of "seeing" another aspect of our planet, and finding another outlet for her love of adventure in the world of caves.

She had read most of my books and we had been in correspondence for some years when we embarked on the series of underground expeditions which she describes. To me her behaviour in circumstances often of extreme difficulty - climbing, crawling, hanging in space, picking our way through and over and under chaotic mazes of rock and boulder, stalagmite and debris—was a constant source of wonderment.

Our method was similar to the one she had used in the mountains. She kept a hand on my rucksack, and I was able to lead her along the most intricate paths with very little need to tell her what to do, so adept was she, and so naturally gifted, in following my every movement. Of course I described the scene to her; but it happened only rarely that I paused to ask, "Are you with me? Are you in touch?" when I could not be sure if she was holding on to me or not.

It is not for me to describe our adventures, which she has done admirably; nor need I give any account of her daily life other than to say that, except during her brief holidays, she works like other people in the noise and tumult of our century, far removed from the contemplation and silence in which she delights. She is a person of natural modesty and gentleness who in her indomitable courage and energy, her overflowing optimism and longing to know and try everything, may well serve as an example to us all.

Norbert Casteret

Contents

Illustrations

Key to Acknowledgements

1 Maurice Guyot
2 Norbert Casteret
3 Jacques Jolfre

Introduction

THIS little book, written as plainly and simply as I am able, is
intended for readers of all kinds; but I would ask the particular
indulgence of expert mountaineers, since in their field I cannot
claim to be more than a novice. And I would ask all those who read
it to do so with their hearts; or better, in a spirit of contemplation
in the deepest sense of the word.

Crystals and cold water, snow, sun and moon, these are so many
pure and luminous symbolic images on which it is proper to meditate. To those who know the mountains I would say that it is not
sight alone that matters, and that I hope to show them other things.
Those who do not know them I hope to teach to love them. The
secret wish of mountaineers is to cause others to share the joys they
discover in the heights.

I was born at Versailles in a humble dwelling very near the palace.
When I was two my eyesight failed almost completely, leaving me
with only a faint perception of light, able to distinguish between
sunshine and darkness like a normal person with their eyes tightly
closed.

My parents taught me a love of Nature, and as a little girl I played
with other children either in the Great Park of Versailles, which was
like my private domain, or on the land adjoining it, where my father
had a vegetable-garden near the pond known as the Pièce d'Eau des
Suisses.

At school I became passionately interested in geology and geography; I dreamed of volcanoes and mountains. My holidays were
spent in a village in the Gatinais, where my younger brother and I
played together in an old quarry. It was there, amid the fields and
woods, that my longing for adventure was born. My love of
mountains grew with the years, with the books that were read to

me and those that I read to myself in braille. But I have always had an intense longing for space and great expeditions.

We are all to some extent imprisoned by life, and the thing we most ardently desire is always slow in coming, so that often we feel that it will never come at all. But with patience and courage, if we want them enough and love them enough, all things come in the end, however long the time may be.

In 1953 I visited my first mountain—a small one certainly, but still a mountain. Providence sometimes arranges things to suit us. I went as a tourist for reasons of health, because I was badly in need of a change from city life, and on 4th August that year I first set foot on the Mer de Glace. My dream of becoming a real climber never afterwards left me. In all of us there is a sleeping star which, consciously or unconsciously, we seek to grasp.

My love of mountains was such that it absorbed all my thoughts, even to the point of wearying me, but it stimulated me as well. My friends, seeing the fascination they had for me, found it hard to understand why. Why go to the mountains, they wondered, when one cannot see them?

It is a large question and a strange one, but one which I find it easy to answer. We do not need to see mountains in order to love them, any more than we need to see, or even hear, a person who is dear to us. Their presence is enough. For me it is enough that mountains exist.

People describe landscapes to me. I picture them, and I note the reactions of my companions, their delight, their exclamations of wonderment when a new prospect is disclosed at a turn in the path. The landscape I imagine may not be the real one; it may be more or less beautiful than the reality; but what does that matter? For me it is real and it possesses its own truth.

I believe strongly in the truth of my inward feeling, and it is the idea I have of things which gives so much *value* to my mountains. Snow, rocks and glaciers, no doubt I idealise all these a little; but if I endow the things and people I love with so many qualities, I recognise their faults as well.

I do not go to the mountains for the same reasons as other climbers, and that is all that can be said. We approach them in a different way. And so people are often surprised by my evocation of the mountains, and my love of them. But sight is only one of our senses.

There are all the things one perceives by other means, things one knows by intuition, things one can hear and touch and smell and taste. In the foothills there are waterfalls, flowers, cattle-bells and raspberries.

What one experiences at higher altitudes is to my mind more precious and rare because it is difficult of access: the wind in the peaks, the footsteps of the rope-party in the snow, the steady crunch of the ice-axe sinking into it, the falling stones which whistle as they fall, avalanches, the sounds coming from the glacier's depths ... And there is also, which is wonderful to me, the reflection of brilliant sunshine on untrodden snow, the warmth, the quiver, the extraordinary light that is to be found nowhere else.

There is the keen, cold air that stings the cheeks, the delicate, almost imperceptible scent of snow which has in it something of pine, of grass and of flowers. There is the use we who are sightless must make of our hands, the feeling of rock and snow.

There is the wonderful comradeship of the climbing-party, the friendship and mutual trust; the atmosphere of the mountain huts where one shelters; the nights of waiting and the mornings of setting out; the plans, the prospects, the difficulties to be overcome on an awkward climb. There are the debates about the weather, which one prays will be perfect, because that is the first requisite if the climb is to be a success.

All these simple matters, which in another book might sound merely commonplace, so much padding, here assume an especial significance. The guide who escorts a blind climber up a mountain is undertaking a great responsibility.

There is the poetry of darkness in the mountains, when the party sets out before the sun has risen. There are all the things I have forgotten to mention, which may be termed the local colour of the mountain peaks.

Why do I climb mountains? Quite simply because the mountains and I had to meet. I go for my pleasure and to conquer myself. I know of nothing more deadly than inaction, whether physical or mental. One needs to try one's strength and one's willpower, to triumph over one's destiny, to remake oneself, to put one's muscles to use.

I do not climb mountains in order to break records of height or altitude. Those things do not interest me. I do it because I love the beauty and simplicity of a way of living which brings confidence, which confirms resolution and calls for courage.

Is it difficult to climb when one cannot see? Is it not more dangerous than for a person possessing sight?

A mountain is a great lady who must not be treated lightly. She is not easily mastered by anyone, still less by a person without eyes. She is in the first place a friend; for friendship is the best of what we give and take from one another. To conquer her calls for great patience and perseverance; one must learn to know her.

In practice one needs to be in good condition, capable of walking for very long stretches, with the least possible fatigue and expenditure of effort, over every kind of surface, rocky for preference. The ideal ground for persons without sight is that of the mule-tracks at an altitude of between 6000 and 8000 feet. I shall come back to this. And it goes without saying that a blind person must always be well escorted, accompanied by experienced guides and team-mates.

Unquestionably climbing is more difficult for a blind person—I mean, climbing in the *high mountains*. It is also more dangerous and entails a greater expense of energy, besides inducing a state of constant nervous tension in every member of the team. One ends by acquiring a certain technique, tricks and devices which one perfects with every climb.

Does blindness induce vertigo? Are the blind more susceptible to heights than normal climbers?

No, I do not think that, lacking sight, one can suffer from vertigo in the ordinary sense of the word—that is to say, see the world spinning round one, so that one is tempted to fling oneself into the void. In this respect the blind have an obvious advantage, although it is one that we would prefer to do without.

My friend Monsieur Arthur Richard of Morzine, who is the only blind Frenchman to have reached the summit of Mont Blanc (21st July, 1959) once said to me, referring to a newspaper article which talked about the extreme perceptiveness of the blind, "Those of us who claim to be conscious of the change of altitude after climbing thirty or forty feet are certainly remarkably sensitive—to the point of making themselves ridiculous. The change is only perceptible in thousands of feet. You know it by a sense of space, a sort of headiness . . . the smell of the air."

The remark is a very interesting one. What Monsieur Richard, a great observer and born mountaineer, calls with so much truth and precision "the smell of the air" is what I would term, more fancifully, "the scent of snow". Although physical vertigo does not exist for us, we may still experience a very strange feeling, a sort of "moral vertigo" if I may so express it. This can be terrible. Certainly it is in part imaginary, and it is something against which one has to fight with all one's strength. Above all one has to keep one's head, behave even more calmly than usual and do nothing capricious (I can see my climbing companions smile as they read those words!), which is not always an easy matter.

Our master once said to us at school, "We see much more with our minds than with our eyes", and the words are perfectly applicable here. One perceives, with all one's senses alert. The mind registers impressions. One has to concentrate without becoming over-strained. Everything varies according to the inner mood, and it is very important to be good-humoured.

The blind are conscious of space. Obviously they cannot measure depth, especially when it is a matter of thousands of feet. But the sense of space has a great effect on them, and it is not always an unpleasant one. It may, on the contrary, be wonderfully exciting. Everything depends at such moments on the general mood of one's team-mates, the coolness and deliberation of those who guide and direct the climb.

I shall return to this matter in talking of my own climbs; but I can say at once that if one is overtaken by that kind of panic at some very unpropitious moment, practice and experience do much to relieve it. I was far more frightened on my first climbs than during the later ones.

As in life, the important thing is to gain the utmost confidence in oneself, and above all to trust the rope which links one to one's comrades. It is also important that they should clearly describe the movements to be made, and the scene in general; but they alone are the judges of this.

I have learnt that for a blind person who attempts mountaineering the two most essential virtues are obedience and trust. I cannot pretend to possess them entirely, a whole lifetime would not be enough for me to acquire them. And what I have said about mountaineering applies equally to exploring the subterranean world. This is not really surprising for the two worlds are one—the mountain and what is hidden in its heart.

PART ONE

ON THE HEIGHTS

I

Climbing-School

WE were on Route 403, which leads to Le Fayet, and my guide,
Louis Piraly of Saint-Gervais, and my friend Raymond, were
discussing our future excursions—such wonderful plans . . .

I was thinking of the high peaks surrounding us, which I already
loved. I knew that they would cost me much suffering and
exertion, but I did not believe that they would disappoint me.

How can one talk of mountains except with passion, with a deep
and overflowing love? Mountains are among the great things on
our earth, those which most fascinate men and cast a spell over
them, like oceans, deserts, caves and the stars.

How think of mountains without thinking of the heroic
climbers who first found the way to their summits—Jacques Balmat,
Dr. Paccard, H.-B. de Saussure, Whymper, Franz Lochmatter,
Heckmair, Michel Croz, Zwingelstein, Louis Lachenal and so
many others—the great men of all nationalities who by their
writings, and in their lives or their deaths, first created and then
did honour to the sport of mountaineering.

The sport—the mystique—was born on the day a man first gazed
up at the white peaks. Of this encounter between the heart of a
man and the heart of the mountains a love was born which nothing
can destroy.

When the tourist and the climber say, "I am going to the
mountains", they are not talking the same language. The first is
thinking of pleasant views and easy slopes, with an undertone
of snobbery in the thought of the great heights he will reach
by cable-car. But the other, the climber, is thinking of the long
day's struggle over glaciers, and however calm he may appear
he is in reality seized with a greater excitement than the mere
sightseer can ever know. The climber has no love of the elbowing
which reminds him of going to the office in the train. To him

there can be no contemplation in a crowd. He prefers a life of near-solitude with one or two companions, as remote as possible from the valleys.

Now that every peak in the Alps has been conquered, the climber looks for new and more difficult ways up them, or sets out to explore more distant ranges, and it is proper that he should. "Let us sound all the walls, try all the paths, survey all the abysses . . ."

The car stopped presently in the park of Le Fayet, the thermal station. Brilliant sunshine, but not many people on the crags, and so much the better! I was roped to Monsieur Piraly; he started the ascent while I awaited my turn. I was a little frightened, naturally. I had done no rock-climbing, or very little. I was afraid that it would be too much for me.

I thought of the advice I had been given—"Be perfectly relaxed, perfectly calm, convince yourself that you're in first-rate condition. There's no reason why you shouldn't make it. Blind people have no difficulty in finding footholds." Very nice in theory! My friends were wonderful. All the same, I needed to take a grip of myself if I was not to start inventing reasons for giving up the attempt.

I should have taken myself in hand a little earlier. The process did not seem to be working very well. But then I said to myself, "Well anyway I'm going to have a shot!" and after that I awaited Piraly's order with a kind of exhilaration that was new to me.

"Come along. But go gently. Be careful of your hand and footholds, and take your time."

A little way off I could hear Yvonne and Pierrette talking. They had said, "We're coming to see how you get on." It seemed that I was bound to try, if only not to disappoint them. So I started.

I had a queer sense of having no strength in my arms, which was perhaps not very surprising as I was tired and not in training; and in any case, all beginners probably feel the same. But it caused me a moment of panic. I thought of what my parents would say if they could see me. I was suddenly terrified. I fumbled my holds, desperately longing to go down again, while I muttered something and Raymond and Piraly shouted encouragement from above.

I had to keep on, or what would Pierrette and Yvonne think, seeing me hanging on the rope? Finally I hoisted myself painfully on to the flat top of the rock.

"Well, since you're so keen on going down again you can do it now!"

So now I was to make a rope-descent, my first. How wonderful! I trembled a little, but that would pass.

"You pass the rope round your right thigh and over your left shoulder. Spread your legs and go backwards, lying more or less horizontal as you pay the rope out. Don't be afraid. You're quite safe."

Faithfully obeying orders I made my first descent, not very cleverly. But I managed it, and the initiation gave me confidence. I stopped trembling and was ready to climb again.

This time it was Raymond who secured me with the safety-rope while Piraly climbed alongside me and guided my hands and feet. One has a great sense of safety with a guide at one's side, and this is another thing that all beginners know.

"You're gripping upside down with your left hand. This is a good rock-face, there are holds everywhere."

"For the hands, yes—but not for the feet."

"Why not for your feet? Try to get them to grip the surface. Your boots won't slip. The soles were made for rock-climbing."

"I keep on slipping. I haven't got the knack."

"The fact is, you aren't trusting those soles. You can't get a hold with the toe or the side of your foot, it's got to be flat on the surface. There, that's better."

Raymond made jesting comments as he watched me climb. I managed somehow or other to get to him, and then started to repeat the descent.

"Spread your legs more!"

But something was going wrong. I swung to the right and did not react quickly enough to recover my balance. I hung there swinging and my body turned so that my back bumped against the rock. It all happened very quickly, and Raymond swore while with an effort he checked my fall.

"It was your own fault. You didn't do as you were told. Have you hurt yourself?"

"No."

Piraly came alongside.

"That'll do for today."

"No, I want to try again."

I knew there was nothing worse than to give up after a failure. If a horse refuses a jump you put him at it again so that he won't do the same thing twice. I was like the horse. I knew myself only too well. If I didn't do it properly now I should never make a good rope-descent, or at least I should always be afraid of them.

The next time I managed it. I got down perfectly and was delighted and enormously relieved.

"That was a very good first lesson," said Piraly. "No need to worry about what happened. It's the same with every beginner."

So after all, I was just a beginner like the rest!

The few days that were left of my holiday were spent in initiating me into rock climbing. We went to the Rocher de l'Escalade. The sun was very hot and there were a lot of other people about, climbers and strollers.

I was roped to Raymond, who led the way to reassure me. Piraly stood watching us at a distance and taking occasional photographs, so I had to find my holds by myself. This was something it was essential for me to learn, because I could not always have an instructor beside me.

It was not as simple as it may seem. I took care only to move one arm or leg at a time, so as not to lose my balance, and I tried to move from one hold to the next smoothly, without jerking. I can't pretend that my style was very good.

I thought of the sort of things people say about the blind— "They have such a wonderfully developed sense of touch! They're so adroit! They have a sixth sense. There's a special god for the blind." And there were also people who would say, "For God's sake, why do they want to go climbing rocks?"

Meanwhile there I was on the rock-face at the end of a rope, and I alone was the judge of my actions because I alone knew what it was all about.

Every climber knows that even a moment's hesitation on the part of one member can throw a rope-team out of its stride. Certainly this was different, since we were only doing a practice climb. But still, without eyes to see one is bound at times to fumble for a few seconds before finding a protruberance which can be firmly grasped.

I had to trust to luck . . . My right hand seized upon a tiny hold, although there was a far better one only a few inches away from it which I could not see; my left hand sought the ideal projection but could not find it, nothing but a small bulge too near for me to be able to use it. Further off a ledge jutted sharply out, but too high for me to be able to hoist myself up to it. I could find nothing between the two. This groping about, which took less time than it takes to write, was enough to make me lose my balance. My feet slipped, and I could not steady myself with my right hand alone. Once again I was hanging on the rope; the more I sought a foothold the more my feet slipped, while my hands fumbled blindly (the right word!) and the rope dug into my ribs. If there had been an instructor beside me he would have told me what to do, but he was down below, watching and saying nothing.

His silence made me cross. I looked up and called: "Raymond, I can't do it, I want to go down."

Raymond knew better than anyone what the position was because he was having to sustain my full weight, but he said calmly: "Well, come on up first, and then we'll see."

He laughed; but my courage was failing and my muscles wouldn't obey me. I had to stop this. I was hot, scorched by the sun.

"Listen, Raymond. Piraly didn't really mean it, did he, when he said I have a natural gift for climbing? He only said it to please me."

"Find somewhere to put your feet and rest for a moment."

"I'm completely out of breath!"

"You're going at it too hard."

His imperturbability restored my morale. I took his advice and rested. Then I made another effort and reached him.

"You mustn't let yourself get so upset," he said. "Don't fuss, you'll get the hang of it. It's bound to take a little time. You aren't doing badly. All you need is practice."

"Are we going down now?"

"Whenever you like."

He gave me a friendly pat on the shoulder, because I was still a little scared when it came to stepping off backwards into emptiness. I knew all about the drop below me, having just climbed up it . . . But having made the first step I felt wonderful. "It's going better now, isn't it?"

I made more short climbs and more descents, economising nervous energy as much as I could so as to be able to control my physical movements and master the fits of nervousness which tended to make me lose strength at the critical moment. One has to forget the emptiness below, which is not dangerous when one is securely roped. One has to have confidence and think only of the climb.

In climbing the hands are at least as important as the feet, if not more so; I was proud of possessing two such fine instruments to replace my eyes.

For further practice we went to another place where the rocks were of limestone. There were fewer holds, but our composition soles gripped well. I began to make progress. The weather and the surroundings both were perfect. But, alas, holidays have to end . . . We had many jokes between us, particularly when Raymond played at being an instructor and climbed without a rope.

"Watch out, I'm on my way down! Spectacular descent!"

He landed on his behind with a bad bruise on his shoulder where he had bumped himself in passing, but still he laughed. He was a great clown. "You're setting me a fine example," I said. Then he made the climb properly, under the amused and watchful eye of Monsieur Piraly.

It is customary among mountaineers to pay tribute to their predecessors, and so I am bound to record that blind persons—all men, I think—have been mountaineers before me.

The first blind man to climb Mont Blanc was, I believe, a Scot; but it happened a long time ago, and I do not know the details. But there is a story told by Guido Rey which I pass on without comment, since I have not been able to confirm the facts and do not know the nationality of the climber or even when the climb took place. Guido Rey wrote:

"A blind man had himself hauled to the summit of the Cervin. When his guides told him that he had reached the highest point he was seized with a great joy. I wish that I could have seen that landscape as it appeared to his sightless eyes. His vision was perhaps more splendid than the real prospect of snow and rock, for he had in his heart the true spirit of the mountains."

Coming nearer to our own time I must not ignore the splendid feat of Monsieur Arthur Richard, to whom I have already referred. On 21st July, 1959, he climbed Mont Blanc from the Nid d'Aigle in *eight hours*, returning the same way, by the normal route of the Aiguille du Gouter.

If you ask Monsieur Richard why he took to mountaineering he replies: "Because I enjoy it, and for exercise. I go purely for pleasure, to test myself in the heights and also to show what a blind person can do." He found the Aiguille du Gouter the most difficult part of the climb.

There were also the blind Rover Scouts in the Pyrenees, who climbed the Pic d'Anie, about 8000 feet.

As to whether there are many blind people capable of becoming mountaineers, or who wish to do so, it is hard to say. Climbing is a dangerous sport to which different people react in different ways. Every climber owes a duty to the others on the rope as well as to himself.

I often find that people have only a vague understanding of the different kinds of mountaineering. We have to distinguish between mule-tracks, relatively climbable rocks, shifting moraines, glaciers and ice-covered slopes. All have beauties of their own. All present their own peculiar difficulties, in which particular climbers specialise.

All human activity is to be judged by the spirit in which it is undertaken. I believe strongly in the impelling power of small things, because they sometimes lead to greater ones. I know very well that all mountaineers are not mystics or poets, but I do not believe that any one who comes under the spell of the mountains can be casual about it. Can any climber, strapped in his "iron-mongery", looking for a way up a vertical or overhanging face and carefully calculating his next step, fail to believe in something greater than himself?

There is a pride in achievement which is not to be confused with mere vanity. There is the happiness of preparation, of struggle, of reward. Are these purely physical joys, or purely a matter of physical sensation? Are the mountains really "a heap of rocks and nothing more" as I have heard them described?

No, there is more than this, the aspiration towards beauty, goodness and greatness, the thirst to explore, the thirst for the Infinite! It adds up to very much more than a heap of rocks.

What climber, standing on a glacier or in the Vallée Blanche, has not felt, as I have, a longing to open his arms, to spread his wings like a great bird? They must be rare indeed, those who have never felt that intoxication of the heights.

To conclude this little dissertation on mountain-climbing, that great educator, I may add that for me the love of mountains is something deeper, more spiritual, mystical and contemplative, than any mere love of sport.

2

Le Mont Tondu

O N the 16th August, 1960, we climbed to the Tré-La-Tête
shelter, a height of about 6000 feet.

The track was an easy one. I went with Monsieur Piraly and the
Abbé Meynet. Meynet was a good friend and a good mountaineer,
and we jokingly called him the apprentice-guide.

Let me say at once that it was not because there was any thought
of death or the last sacrament in our minds that we had brought
a priest with us. On the contrary, we were all in high spirits, and
Meynet had come simply for the pleasure of doing so. In these
days a great many priests take up mountaineering, following the
example of Pope Pius XI, who wrote admirably on the subject
and has left us the beautiful form of benediction for ropes and
ice-axes.

We reached the shelter at about five on a beautiful summer
evening, and I was wildly happy. We had talked all the way,
telling tales of guides and accidents, of which there is never any
lack, and joking and laughing and thoroughly enjoying ourselves.
There had been no hurry, and Piraly had stopped here and there
to gather mushrooms. The undergrowth smelt of damp earth,
humus and moss. A party of about a dozen climbers had passed us,
also making for the shelter, which meant that we should have
plenty of company.

Towards the end of the climb the track narrowed and we had
to go in single file, taking care where we put our feet. The air
was growing cooler, and we could hear in the distance the tinkling
of cow-bells. When we reached the shelter Piraly stood on the
verandah telling us the names of the peaks to be seen on the
horizon. He knew them all, and each one had its history. Meynet
and I greatly admired his erudition, although, of course, it was
part of a guide's job, and one of the most delightful, it must be said.

31

We went inside. I was enormously hungry. We dumped all our equipment in a corner, rucksacks, anoraks, jerseys, ropes and ice-axes. It is what every climber does when he comes stamping into a shelter, but to me it was wonderful.

We were greeted by other guides who told us of the expeditions they and their parties were planning for the morrow. They were men from Gervais and the Contamines, and I liked their sing-song accents. One party was going on to the Bérangère, another to the Miages and others to l'Infranchissable or, like ourselves, to the Mont Tondu, the Shorn Mountain.

The great question was the weather, but everyone was sure it would be fine. We had to turn in early, because the alarm-clock was set for three in the morning.

It was a long time before I fell asleep . . . There have been many tragedies in the Massif of Tré-La-Tête—that of the Skier, of the youthful party from the Contamines and of the Dutchmen. Everyone knew about them, but all hoped that this time the Great Lady would be kind. Well, I had Piraly and Meynet to look after me, and there could be no better escort. Still, this was my first real climb in the high mountains. A real glacier, and a big one, was no laughing matter. But it was what I had been dreaming of all my life. I was twenty-five years old—why should I not succeed?

When the alarm went off I seemed scarcely to have slept at all. I carefully dusted my feet and ankles with talcum powder—they had a hard day's work ahead of them!—and laced my heavy boots.

Piraly and Meynet took nothing but black coffee, saying that one climbs better on an empty stomach. It may be so, but all the same I ate three slices of bread-and-butter and drank two glasses of strong tea.

In the general-room of the shelter people were talking doubt-fully about the weather. It was not cold enough, they said, and the sky threatened rain, which meant snow at the higher altitudes. But Piraly was not worried.

"We're going, my children. It'll be fine. The clouds will lift at ten."

We set off at four o'clock, to be plunged into the silence and poetry of darkness on the mountains. There was a soft, moist breeze.

Meynet felt cold. He was seriously afraid of bad weather and he had not brought an anorak. We teased him, and then Piraly went back to the shelter to get him one. I was reminded of the scolding I had been given for setting out for the mountains without a raincoat. I was tempted to laugh, but I thought it tactful not to say anything. All was well with Meynet once he had the anorak on. Piraly was full of optimism, and his experience as chief of rescue-parties for that district made him a reliable judge of the weather. I trusted him to guide my footsteps and felt sure I should not regret doing so.

We were going up the Tré-La-Tête glacier, but first we followed its left-hand lateral moraine. Piraly remarked in passing: "This is where the three Dutchmen were killed last year. One slipped and the other two lost their grip. They were found on the glacier two hundred feet below."

We proceeded in Indian file, taking extreme care. I bumped now and then against the rocky wall on my left, which sometimes overhung us and from which water constantly dripped. The face was scored by the progress of the glacier in reaching its present level. Nearly all the European glaciers have moved downwards since the beginning of this century, and Tré-La-Tête was no exception. The fact is striking when one considers the deep gorge at its mouth, and I recalled a sentence I had read: "A glacier is a river of ice which tends to sharpen the contours and reliefs of its bed, instead of smoothing them as flowing water does."

Gradually we worked our way down the moraine until we reached the glacier. It was dirty here, littered with stones and debris. We moved along it, always keeping to the left side, for nearly a mile. Piraly told us about the formation of the *moulins*, circular holes caused by melt-water bubbling up to the surface. The water swirls round in these wells with an impressive, roaring sound, and can be heard at great depths. The glacier at this point was about a thousand feet deep.

We now roped ourselves, and for the next few hours our fortunes would be linked for better or for worse. Holding our ice-axes in our right hands and the rope with our left we advanced steadily and slowly, making precise, careful movements.

"The first time one is roped for a climb one has a drink to celebrate," said Piraly. I said nothing, having been roped before.

We veered presently to the right to avoid the dangerous zone

of seracs, huge, over-hanging ice-masses liable to fall at any time.
The day had now dawned, shyly and hesitantly, and a light wind
was blowing. It was pleasant to hear our feet crunch on the untrodden snow. I had a feeling that mine were treading a path they
had been always destined to tread. I was in my natural element,
and a feeling of wild joy possessed me—the joy of surpassing
oneself, of freedom, of profound peace. Names rang in my ears—
Tré-La-Tête, la Grande Muraille, la Bérangère, La Lex-Blanche
(so sadly celebrated). Yesterday Odette, Yvonne and Rolande had
said to me, "Will you think of us when you're up there?"

The very bad snow conditions of that year of 1960 were not
making things easy for us; there was two feet of fresh snow. We
were slowly gaining height, but it would require great staying-
power to reach the Tondu.

Piraly was first on the rope and I was in the middle; this was
real climbing. Now and then we had to jump a crevasse, or go
round the ones which were too wide for me, which took longer
but was less hazardous.

"Here's another narrow one," said Piraly. "Put your foot there,
on the edge—a bit further, beside mine." He held my left hand
while I used my ice-axe to measure the width of the crevasse.
"Right—jump!"

The glacier was exactly as I had imagined it to be. I did not
feel at all strange. I felt that I was coming to love the mountains
more and more, but that I should need great courage.

Here and there Piraly tested the depth of the snow with the
handle of his ice-axe to make sure that it did not conceal a hidden
crevasse. We proceeded for the most part in silence, but at intervals
Meynet talked about the difficulties he had encountered on a
previous climb, and this became the main topic of the day.

On the far right of the glacier we followed a moraine path of
small loose rock fragments. For me this part of the climb was
very difficult and dangerous. I did not know where to put my feet.
The stones constantly shifted under my weight, and I had great
trouble in keeping my balance. I made constant use of my hands,
feeling the stones to make sure of their firmness before setting
foot on them. I was nearly always either on all fours or crouching.
Those wretched stones caused us to lose a lot of time. Although
we were roped I had to solve my own problems, for the guide's

function was to lead the way and shift stones that were obviously unsafe. Meynet, behind me, gave me what guidance he could in placing my feet; he was very patient.

We had not yet devised methods to enable us to get along faster. Piraly was not used to leading the blind, still less in the mountains, and this was only too clear. I did not yet know him very well, and I was afraid of making too many suggestions. It would all sort itself out in time. I was convinced that I should return to the mountains. I knew it. But it would never be easy for me . . .

Truly, happiness is not achieved by doing things easily. Later climbs were to seem to me at times more difficult than anything I had read about; but there were other times when they seemed simpler.

I tried to follow my natural instincts. There was a kind of tenseness about our rope-party of which we were all conscious in varying degrees. For Piraly it was a matter of pride to get me up Mont Tondu, and also he wanted to please me, and anyway it was his job. He may have had his doubts about it, but he was very anxious to succeed. As for Abbé Meynet, he was simply there to help, and he did his best to be useful. In a way he was at the opposite extreme from Piraly—happy to be making this climb for the second time.

For myself, I was going to the Tondu to carry to its peak the tiny flame in my heart.

We continued to gain height, and the loose, rough surface went on and on. It seemed to me interminable and it was exhausting. I was not happy, because I could not help realising how easy it would be to break a limb on the unstable path. I tried to avoid letting the rope drag on the ground in case it got frayed—it was a good perlon rope—and I took particular care to avoid getting my feet caught in it.

"Would you like a drink?" asked Piraly.

"Yes, I would, rather. The air's very dry."

"We're getting on," he said. "We've lost a bit of time on the moraine, but we'll get there. We aren't doing too badly, all things considered."

Was he laughing at me or trying to cheer me up? He was certainly trying to encourage me. The people of Savoy seldom pay compliments. I remembered how he had said, "You have a talent for rocks," at the climbing-school.

Over to our left we could hear the rattle of stones as they plunged down on to the glacier. Otherwise there was complete silence.

We were now at a height of about 8000 feet and there was snow in the chinks between the stones. I had to be doubly careful because the coating made them very slippery. If my feet were not thoroughly educated after this exercise, they never would be!

But nobody felt like laughing. Piraly talked in an encouraging tone, indicating the best path. I don't know how I managed not to scrape all the skin off my hands on those sharp edges of rock; it was almost miraculous.

"Well, that's over," said Piraly.

At last we were all together again.

We went gently, very gently, up the long slope of fresh-fallen alpine snow, no sound but the scrape of the ice-axes on the rock beneath. All my life I had dreamed of holding an ice-axe in my hand, but now there was no time for dreaming, because the mountain allowed me no respite. The slope grew steeper and finally very steep. At every step one had to make an effort to plant one's foot securely in the snow.

I tried to find a method. The best was to feel the way with my hands, so I resumed my painful progress, bent double. We were all breathing deeply, matching our movements to the rhythm of our breath. Piraly helped me by making good big footprints in which I put my feet.

The snow was beginning to burn my fingers. It was time to put on the gloves Rolande had given me before I set out. We were now on a long rope, at some distance from each other. It was very hard going, the stretch of soft snow seemed endless. If the surface had been harder I could have put on crampons. Weariness was beginning to overcome me. I sat down in the snow, but Meynet called me to order.

"You can stand still and rest for a minute on an ascent, but you must never sit down. If you do your legs get stiff and you find it harder than ever."

It was a little past eight in the morning when we reached the Col des Chasseurs, at a height of nearly 10,000 feet. This was the only spot on that particular climb where we could allow ourselves to stop for a short time and have something to eat.

The day was fine but very cold. I had no appetite at all. All I wanted was to rest and drink great gulps of iced tea out of the leather flask. To keep going I forced myself to swallow some bread and ham.

My spirits revived. We passed through other steep, endless snowfields and I went on all fours, finding this the most effective and least tiring method. I wanted to live the present moment as intensely as possible. My companions were plunged in their own thoughts—to get to the summit . . . I wanted to experience for a few moments the sense of tremendous solitude in the presence of the mountains, to feel quite alone, remote from everything, a thousand miles from civilisation . . . But it did not happen. That spiritual state was denied me, and I was rather sad.

Things turn out strangely. Sometimes in the valleys of men, when one is surrounded by people, one feels horribly alone; but here, on the 17th August, 1960, at a height of 10,000 feet, I could not feel alone. Why was it? Down below, at the chalet, they must be thinking of our party—that is the great human fellowship. Yet scarcely anyone knew that this morning we were on the Tondu. So . . .?

We had to make a short traverse to the left—just when I thought our troubles were over. Piraly went ahead to secure us. I did not like our being widely separated, because as a rule we were closely roped, but here it was necessary. Meynet was some yards behind me. We went very cautiously, wholly concentrated on the business of putting hands and feet in the right places, while Piraly watched us.

"Take it easy. It's slippery."

"Listen, Piraly," said Meynet. "If Colette loses her grip what do I do? It must be a two-hundred-foot drop."

"At least!"

Meynet was really marvellous. My position was certainly a strange one, my feet in two small toe-holds, my fingers clutching icy rock, my face turned up to the sun, which had just appeared. I did not move; I held my breath so as to hear better. I had a feeling that I was trembling and that my fingers were slipping. I was frightened. The blood was pounding in my veins. I felt—or better still, I heard—the void on my left.

(As all blind people know, it is our ears that enable us to perceive a wall, or a break in a wall at a street-crossing, because they sense the thickness of the air in relation to a fairly close solid object.)

Yet in my heart I was glad to be feeling this fear, this anguish of terror, because to do so is to be vulnerable. All climbers know it from time to time, and one needs to know it at least once in one's life, because all other fears seem trifling in comparison.

"Everything all right?" asked Piraly.

"Yes, but I wouldn't want it to go on too long."

"Well, hang on. I'm going to take a photograph. A formidable slope with a crevasse at the bottom—you'll look splendid!"

This was pure Piraly and it produced a burst of laughter from us both. Those seconds seemed very long, but I forgot to be afraid, I was laughing so much.

"Now move, Colette!"

The sharp order restored my calm, but I still did not move a finger. The rope grew taut—I had to move at all costs. Sentences ran through my mind like sparks blown from God knew where—"Courage is to be afraid and be the only one that knows it . . . If you were never afraid what would be the use of courage?"

I mastered myself and moved on until I had come up with Piraly. Then we repeated the process. It was a long, slow business. My companions were fortunate since they could see our objective, the summit, and reckon how far we had to go. I could not, and that made it much harder. The summit meant little to me until I was on it.

A small outcrop of rock bothered me. "What shall I do?" I asked Meynet.

"You must sort it out for yourself. I'm hanging on by my eyelids, and I'm not a bit keen on falling."

"Really, Colette," said Piraly, "what a way to climb! I thought I'd taught you not to hang on with your knees."

It was tough going for my companions as well as for me. I was like a baby which wants the walk to be over, and I surprised myself by asking: "How much longer is this going on?"

The silence had become heavy and solemn. The sun warmed me. We took several photographs. We had been seven hours on the ascent (two and a half hours longer than the normal time) but the snow conditions were very bad and I was lacking in experience.

We reached the terminal ridge, which was long and snowy. A

friendly rope-party passed us in the opposite direction, greeting us with shouts of encouragement. Now that victory was so close I ventured to sit down and rest, and Piraly said that for a person who could not see any climb must be considered twice the effort, so I had really done it twice over.

At last we were at the summit, 3196 metres, by French reckoning. It was an unforgettable moment, an immediate reward for all our efforts. I felt compensated for all the troubles in my life, a life so well worth living.

I embraced my guide. Within myself I tried to evoke the great silence which is an act of immense thanksgiving. I thought of my parents, my family, the friends who would never see this spot, and indeed were far from supposing that on this morning, at eleven o'clock, I was treading the snow at a height of 10,000 feet.

We were surrounded by high mountains which Piraly named for us. The Italian frontier was not far off and we thought of Mont Rose, about 15,000 feet. Where we stood was like the end of the world. I longed to see all the peaks, but perhaps if I did I should love them less. Things are very well as they are.

The sky was clouding over.

"Quick, Meynet," said Piraly, "You take the lead. Colette, you keep beside me. Dig your heels well in."

"I'm slipping."

"Go carefully."

The slight alarm I felt climbing down the steep slope of the ridge was instantly dispelled on the Tondu glacier, which I glissaded down—it was glorious! The sheer intoxication of sliding! Those were unforgettable minutes which will brighten all my life. A blind girl on the Tondu glacier! And Meynet produced a splendid phrase: "The mountains are wonderful on the way down!"

We laughed like mad creatures, happy and proud of our hard-won victory. Only God can measure the worth of our effort.

In moments of great fatigue during the ascent by the other route that morning, I had now and then found myself counting my footsteps—"One for mummy—one for auntie—one for so-and-so . . ."—like a child being made to eat its soup.

"All the same, it was a difficult climb," said Piraly.

"Yes, and now it's over."

"If we were to do it again you'd find it much easier—there wouldn't be the fear of the unknown."

"I'm sure you're right—but perhaps it would be less wonderful."

"Watch out, we're in the avalanche area. I can see there's been a new fall—it must have happened after that party we passed half an hour ago went by."

In the pocket of my anorak I was clutching a small pebble which will always be precious to me, for I picked it up on the summit of Mont Tondu and it is the souvenir of a great adventure.

3

The White Valley

IT was eight o'clock on the morning of the 23rd August, 1960, when Monsieur Piraly, his fourteen-year-old daughter Chantal and my friend Raymond came to pick me up at the chalet. The day promised to be brilliantly fine, and we were all happy to be meeting again for another excursion.

From Chamonix we went by cable-car to the Aiguille du Midi. It was a joy to be at a height of 12,000 feet, bathed in the keen air and sunshine which are characteristic of those altitudes. Here, as on other summits, climbers have done reverence to the Virgin Mary by naming her image "Our Lady of the Peaks".

I know this place, having been here two years before with my father, when we were on our way to Italy by the Vallée Blanche cable-line.

Today we were again going to Italy, but although we should again be traversing the Vallée Blanche, we should be going on foot this time, instead of flying over it. To get down into that great glacial bowl one follows the rope-line from the Aiguille du Midi along the Midi-Plan ridge. I am profoundly grateful to the early climbers who established that route before the days of cable-railways.

As we left the Aiguille behind the noise of the cable engines grew increasingly muffled, although the little cars were passing, three at a time, over our heads. While paying careful attention to what I was doing, I tried to take stock of what was going on inside me.

The state of moral vertigo—that is to say, the fear of heights which one has to strive to master—is related to atmospheric conditions, the general atmosphere of the rope-party, and fatigue.

The wind was very cold. The snow had the effect of deadening everything, creating a sort of uniformity, for the ears and the whole

41

being, in which there were no sharp echoes. It was the first time I had been on that ridge, and I could not imagine it very well. I pictured a gentle slope on my right and a precipitous one on my left. In fact it is steep on both sides, towards Chamonix and towards the Vallée Blanche.

It seemed to me that today a blind climber could very well make the descent of the Midi-Plan without being aware of the height. But there was my guide keeping close to me in case I made any mistake, and there were my companions, who were not wholly at ease and at least as much novices as I was myself. However, today there was no need to worry about fatigue, so in general conditions were excellent.

Should one describe the scene to a blind person, or refrain from doing so for fear of alarming them?

It depends on the individual, his state of fatigue and the degree of nervous tension induced by the effort he has had to make, far greater than in the case of an ordinary climber. The guide is the only judge, which means that he needs to know his pupil, or client, very well.

In my own case I very much prefer to know all about my surroundings, with as much detail as possible.

"The track's good and wide here. You can go ahead. There's no danger." Or—"Follow the rope carefully and lean a little to the right." And for my personal satisfaction I like to have an idea of the height. Whether it is 2000 or 10,000 feet obviously makes no difference, since I cannot see the void below me; but I like to know, simply for the record.

There would be no point in taking a blind person into the mountains without telling him exactly what is going on. He is one of the rope-team and he has to play his part in it. To guide a blind person in the mountains, as in daily life, calls for foresight. You need to be quick with advice (without overdoing it), simple, and not afraid to speak plainly. You know that your friend is blind and so does he. You have to work together to make him as little blind as possible.

To lend another person one's eyes is an act of charity and love. The gift is in everyone's power. All that is needed is a little intelligence, and that you should be aware of what you are doing. It does not call for poetry or fine phrases, but for a sense of reality:

and it is this picture of reality, superimposed on the images which the blind make for themselves, that bring them life and happiness.

Yes, it is all the pictures I have received, concentrated and amplified, which cause me to live so intensely in the mountains. Those joys are among the greatest in my life. Even if the truth has sometimes put me in a "blue funk", I have always managed to master my panic in the end. There was the moment on the Mont Tondu when I sat down on the snow because I was exhausted and Meynet's sharp admonishment brought me to my senses.

"You're crazy! One never sits down on a ridge on a steep slope."

"I didn't know we were on a ridge."

Chantal and I went glissading down the Vallée Blanche, and it was rapture. The sun was blazing. We shed our anoraks and jerseys, knowing that in spite of suntan-lotion we should get our arms thoroughly burnt. But I also knew that my bronzed and tanned face would arouse more envy at the chalet than even the visit to the Vallée Blanche.

Piraly was machine-gunning us with his colour-camera; I felt at home in the Vallée Blanche, in my natural element. The silence and the light! I thanked Heaven for having at least left me capable of guessing its whiteness.

There was a riot of mountains all round us, each more beautiful than the last, and Chantal and Raymond were overwhelmed. Piraly named them for us in a calm, matter-of-fact voice (not that he is blasé, for he loves them)—Aiguille du Midi (the Needle of the Midi), Aiguille du Plan, le Mont Blanc du Tacul, le Cardinal, l'Evêque, le Moine, la Nonne (the Bishop, the Monk and the Nun) . . . Lower down, the track passed close to a mined area carefully prepared by ice-technicians—too carefully for our liking. We did not enjoy finding such things on our path, however great their scientific value may be.

Someone waved to us from below. It was Monsieur Blanc, another guide, who was making for the Peigne with a client in tow. We exchanged friendly greetings at a distance and went our separate ways.

"What's that cross?"

"It marks a German cemetery, soldiers who were killed in the last war. There was hard fighting round here. We French were on the Col du Midi."

When a man starts telling war stories there's no stopping him. I walked beside Piraly, sometimes giving him my arm and sometimes holding his rucksack. This expedition was certainly ten times easier than the Tondu.

"Look at those youngsters over there," said Piraly. "They aren't roped."

"You're very rash," we shouted to them. "Where's your rope?"

"No need," they answered laughing. "There aren't any holes in the Vallée Blanche."

And then Raymond suddenly vanished up to his waist. A snow-bridge had given way beneath him, disclosing a deep fissure. It was an alarming moment.

"Keep the rope taut," said Piraly calmly, "and keep going, we don't want to hang about here. That proves that there certainly are holes and that it's necessary to be roped."

The laughing party were some distance off by now, too far away to have learnt anything from our experience. They had had the luck to be lighter than Raymond, that was all.

This reminds me of a rather similar incident reported by a guide from Chamonix, which took place in the Vallée Blanche in 1959.

"I was taking a party to the Col du Géant and we met three young men, unroped, carrying their ice-axes under their arms. 'You ought to rope yourselves,' I shouted to them. They didn't answer. They just laughed and shrugged their shoulders, and I heard one of them say, 'What does he take us for? You'd think we didn't know the difference between a crevasse and a windmill!' So I said to myself, 'Another time, my lad, you'll keep your advice to yourself.' And a few minutes later there was a shout for help. I looked round and saw two of them standing at the edge of a crevasse. The third had fallen in, the one carrying the rucksack with the rope. Well, of course, I went back and hauled him out, although it was quite a job. And when he was on top again, and all intact, I said to him, 'Well, which was it, a crevasse or a windmill?' "

Here and there Piraly tested the depth of the snow. We crossed the fragile snow-bridges one at a time, keeping the rope taut. It was not difficult for me; I simply had to follow in line.

The sun was scorchingly hot and there was no shade at all. We took countless photographs in that setting which is like nowhere else in the world, like a petrified ocean dominated by the Dent du Géant, the Giant's tooth, rising proudly above her sister-peaks.

Chantal was very tired, she had found it hard going. To plough one's way through billows of soft snow under a relentless sun is a laborious and tedious business. I myself had been afraid when we set out that I should be exhausted, because I had given myself no rest since our last excursion; I had been too busy training and practising. But all was well with me; my muscles were in good shape and I felt capable of going on for miles.

We started up the long slope of the Col du Géant, where skiers were having the time of their lives. How wonderful to ski in mid-summer! Just for the fun of it I put on crampons and found the snow excellent.

We met an old Chamonix guide, Alfred Couttet, escorting two climbers. He was obviously glad to see me. He had heard about me, and he told me how delighted he was, now that he was getting on in life, to meet a blind girl who so loved the mountains.

We stopped for refreshment at the old Torino shelter, where we were most warmly received. We were now in Italy and every-thing seemed perfect. The guide from Saint-Gervais, Monsieur Blanc, joined us with his client, and we drank to each other from a bottle of Asti while we talked about the Vallée Blanche, where the thickness of the ice in some places exceeds 2500 feet.

Raymond talked about "his" crevasse, of which the depth must have been considerable, to judge by its gaping mouth adorned with long candles of blue ice. This topic cropped up throughout the day, for he was very proud of his small mishap, and the people of the Midi, as everyone knows, make a point of exaggerating.

But we also talked of Louis Lachenal, who lost his life in the Vallée Blanche in November, 1955, and I cannot end this chapter without a reference to that very great mountaineer.

Louis Lachenal remains one of the greatest of our youthful heroes, for he was an exceptionally skilful climber with indomitable energy. He could only live in the mountains and was happy nowhere else. Let us not forget that he was the first conqueror of Annapurna, a height of 25,000 feet, and with Lionel Terray, his inseparable companion, formed one of the greatest rope-teams in the world. Together they climbed the most formidable northern faces in the Alps.

I know that Louis Lachenal is cherished as an example by a whole generation, and that our young people, who are sometimes called ungrateful, still hold him in deep gratitude. I remember that in August, 1957, among the clusters of moss and pansies on his modest grave in Chamonix, there was a small bunch of edelweiss, put there, if I remember rightly, by Rover Scouts from Douai, in the north of France.

We should like to be able to write and realise the words Louis Lachenal uttered, which constitute a whole way of life: "To live in the mountains, of the mountains."

4

Argentières

I WAS longing to return to the Massif de Tré-La-Tête, which had been the scene of my first climb. But we were out of luck. Rain was reported on the morning of 16th August, 1961, when we had hoped to go. The weather had been atrocious all the first half of August, and we had had to cancel a number of plans.

"I'm sick of vegetating in the chalet, or at the 6000 level," I said to Piraly. "If it's raining over the Contamines it may be fine somewhere else—for instance, at Chamonix. It's depressing to be always putting things off. The holidays slip by and you haven't done a thing. Aren't there any climbs I could manage round Chamonix?"

"Perhaps, but we should have gone up to a high-level shelter yesterday."

"Another day wasted!"

"What do you say to the Petite Aiguille Verte? You'd learn a lot from it."

"Where is it?"

"Above Argentières."

"All right, let's go there. I like the name—Little Green Needle!"

The sky was heavy when we reached Argentières, but it was not raining. We passed the waterfall and began the climb to the shelter at Lognan.

"Is there some kind of work going on here? There seems to be a lot of rubble about."

"There're building a cable-line for skiers."

"Is Lognan a long way?"

"A few hours."

We climbed very slowly up the narrow path, crossing a number of the small streams that issued from the glacier. I was spellbound again by the poetic charm of the rocks and the tranquil forest, of which the scent was stronger than ever under the rain. For it was raining here as well, but we pressed on notwithstanding. I was not going to suggest turning back, leaving it to Piraly to decide if he thought it necessary.

The conditions were strange. We passed through banks of mist and patches of sunshine at different stages as we gained height.

"One doesn't know what to make of this chancey weather," I said. "If you stay at home it's fine, and if you start to go anywhere it rains."

My ice-axe jarred against the rocks, but I was gaining skill with every climb. I walked behind Piraly, holding on to his rucksack, so that I could tell from his movements whether he was going up or down or scrambling over a boulder, and he had no need to warn me, which saved trouble.

But we talked a great deal about matters connected with climbing—famous climbs, rescues, pathfinders and great climbers; about Janu, and Cho-Oyu and his tragedy with Madame Claude Kogan (we did not always agree). A sentence of Renan came into my head—"To the truly philosophical mind everything is equally worthy of being known." One thing led to another, and we uttered lofty reflections on the end of the world and the resurrection of the dead.

It came on to rain very hard and we sat down to rest under the shelter of a pine tree. Then the rain eased and we went on up to Lognan but did not stop there, because by now the sun was brilliantly shining. I shed my thick jersey.

Two goats with tinkling bells accompanied us as far as the moraine of the Argentières glacier, of which we climbed the right-hand side, roping ourselves for greater safety. We passed a rope-party which had turned back—a bad sign.

We had reached a good height when heavy sleet began to fall. It had turned cold. I should have liked to put my jersey on again, but now it was soaked. The cold and damp seeped in under my anorak.

"I wonder what the weather's like in the valley."

"It must certainly be raining."

But why think of the valley when the glacier was calling to me and pleased me infinitely more? Life in the towns had become too heavy and oppressive. The mountains, even under rain, provided an escape from the great prison below, if only for a few hours.

"Hey—what happened to you then?"

"I slipped."

"You know, I'm afraid—" said Piraly.

"You're afraid we shan't make the Little Green Needle today?"

"Well—it's starting to snow. It's eleven o'clock. Let's at least shelter under that rock and have something to eat."

"All right. We really are out of luck, aren't we? This is being a rotten year. And I'm not hungry."

Snow fell on my slice of bread-and-meat and got in under the hood of my anorak. The flakes were getting more and more dense. We were both rather silent.

I picked up my ice-axe as I got to my feet. The blade was horribly cold, and I had a sense of foreboding. The valley was several hours away. Yet I had a great affection for the snow that was preventing me from reaching the summit. It's so different, snow under the sun, but it is perhaps less beautiful because less alive.

While taking care not to slip I let my thoughts wander in inward meditation. The greatest proof of love of the mountains, even of the humblest peak, is acceptance. God had for a moment made use of my small life as a means of showing that we can love in many ways.

We stopped for a short time at Lognan while we had something hot to drink, and met a charming receptionist and a party of German climbers playing cards.

We were back in Chamonix by three, and the sun was almost stifling! This was decidedly a day of ups and downs. So I said to Piraly: "Suppose we took a cable-car up the Aiguille du Midi, and then went down and climbed to the Midi-Plan ridge? Wouldn't that be good practice?

"We can try."

We were lucky in not having to wait long for a car, and presently found ourselves back at the altitude of 12,000 feet. It was a year since I had been there, but this time things were very different. For one thing, it was four in the afternoon, and also there was a very strong wind and we were plunged in mist. All the same, we roped ourselves.

"Where are your gloves?" asked Piraly.

"In my pocket, but I don't want to put them on, they make it so difficult for me to hold my ice-axe."

"Put them on at once!"

It was perfectly obvious, no getting away from it, that I was in one of my panics. I tried to pull myself together, but it wasn't easy. I knew the ridge, and it was nothing terrible. If I let my heart fail me Piraly would be furious at having been brought up there for nothing, and afterwards I should be furious with myself for not having even tried.

"Well, are we going?" said Piraly. "I'll lead. It's better, as there are only two of us. If I let you go first you might miss the track. Hang on to the rope and dig your ice-axe well in."

Up on the ridge the wind was very strong indeed. I didn't know what direction it was coming from, but I couldn't have cared less. The one thing certain was that there was nothing to get in its way —no hope of pretending that we weren't surrounded by empty space.

"I'm scared stiff," I said.

"What do you mean, you're scared stiff? This is no time for being scared."

"I'm afraid of slipping."

"What do you you think the rope's for? And dig in your ice-axe close to your feet, not a couple of yards away."

"I can't seem to manage it."

"Do as you're told."

Piraly plodded on. The ridge was now sloping downward. I was anxious not to get off the track and not to let go of the rope round his waist. All the same, I had to let go and I started to move in a circle.

"For the love of everything, stop spinning round!"

"I've dug my ice-axe in too deep. I can't pull it out."

"For the Lord's sake! Pull it out straight, in a proper manner!"

I realised that the only thing for me to do was not to let Piraly get too far away from me and to walk exactly in his tracks. I didn't say anything more. I concentrated and got on better. We continued the descent, and it got more and more slippery. I said to myself, "Keep calm. You know this ridge."

Conditions were entirely different from last year. That is what the mountains are: one has to adapt oneself and take them as one finds them. I was happy at having again to struggle against fear. But I had had eight hours of walking and climbing, and I was tired even if I didn't feel it.

Last year we had been a party of four, relaxed, setting out on our excursion with the guide in the rear. Now there were only two of us and the guide was in front. It was necessary in my case; and it was nothing but a training exercise, taking place at the end of the day.

Last year we had been on this spot in the morning, and the weather had been fine, with a gentle breeze. Now we were in mist and the bitter wind cut through to our bones.

The snow was freezing over and my feet kept slipping. I couldn't get the point of my ice-axe to go in properly. The lower we got the worse it became.

We were somewhere in the middle of the ridge.

"We need crampons to go any further," said Piraly. "We shall have to turn back."

"All right, but how do we turn?"

"It's not difficult. The track's wide enough. Dig your feet well in. We'll turn right."

We did so.

"Aren't you cold?" asked Piraly.

"Rather the opposite."

"It must be about ten below zero. We don't want to hang about here."

"Am I keeping to the track and following properly in your footsteps?"

"Try keeping a little more to the right, the ground's firmer. Can you feel the emptiness?"

"No, nothing at all, because of the mist, I suppose. It's strange how different everything is."

"Watch out for your feet."

"Well, don't go so fast."

"How can I possibly go fast with you hanging on to me? Give me a bit more room."

"I feel as though my face was on fire."

"And my fingers are numb with working the rope round my alpen-stock. When I think that I had to talk like a sergeant-major to make you put on your gloves!"

The cable-cars bore us through patches of fog and sunshine back to Chamonix, where there was something like a heat-wave. What a day! And what a sport!

"All the same, I'm very happy," I said.

"You find life easier down here?"

It was a different world, that was all.

5

The Red Dog

AFTER a few days of rest and one of training, we set out on a decidedly bold venture. I had my doubts, as I told my companions, but they had made up their minds.

"It's dreadful that I should always be holding you back," I said.

"There's no reason why we shouldn't make it. Besides the weather seems to have turned fine, and—"

"I'm afraid I may not be—"

"Not up to it? We've heard that one before. It's what you always say."

"Very well, then—I'll say no more."

It was 22nd August, 1961. I was not very keen, I must admit. I was glad to be going on a climb, but there was not the same thrill as on other occasions. Perhaps it was better like this. Too much enthusiasm at the start may end in a terrible let-down. If I started in cold blood the climb itself would warm me up. I should certainly learn more from it and perhaps enjoy it more in the end.

We reached Chamonix later than we had planned, Piraly having been warned to stand by for a rescue operation. On the way we collected Maurice, a tall, likeable boy with a northern accent and unfathomable thoughts, but extremely talkative and always smiling.

At two-thirty we set foot on the Mer de Glace, the Sea of Ice, after climbing down the narrow ladders.

"It's freezing!" I said. "What an awful wind!"

"Poor little thing! And it's going to take us five hours to reach the Couvercle shelter."

"I think we shall be fooling ourselves if we don't allow more than that," I said calmly.

"You see, Piraly, she's really pleased. She's protesting for the sake of form—very feminine!"

"How you do talk, my dear Maurice!"

In the event I turned out to have been right. It took us six and a half hours to reach the Couvercle, a heavenly spot amid the "needles". The hours seemed endless as we climbed and traversed the glacier, whose long undulations took all the strength out of my legs. It was dirty, covered with debris, and I cannot pretend that I liked it. Yet I had dreamed of that glacier for a long time and this was my second visit to it, although my first as a climber.

The sun vanished, and the wind pierced anoraks and jerseys. We jumped or circled small crevices in search of less slippery paths. My companions were extraordinarily patient and I admired them greatly. Maurice never stopped talking.

"Watch out—a step forward— there's a hollow here—now up . . . Come this way, it'll be easier for you. Follow me carefully— that's it . . ."

"Aren't you taking any photos?"

"Not worth it. You ought to put on your gloves."

"I don't like wearing gloves."

"Obstinate wench!"

I had fallen several times without hurting myself, but now I scraped my hand on the ice and it bled.

"Now do you see?" cried Maurice.

I put on my gloves and we went on in silence, for a long time keeping to the edge of a stream which had carved a deep channel in the glacier. This was our Ariadne's thread. Finally we were able to cross it by means of a big rock which served as a bridge.

Maurice had fallen silent, and to liven things up I quoted a phrase that had suddenly come into my head.

" 'Mountaineering is a private journey towards an inward truth.' "

"Who said that?"

"I don't know."

"Neither do I."

What were the others thinking about? Certainly of getting to the moraines as quickly as possible. Moraines! . . . Frontal moraines, out of which the torrents spring; bottom moraines; lateral moraines and medial moraines, resulting from a confluence of glaciers . . . That's what the mountains are. I don't like moraines, but one has to cope with them.

"The Drus are over to the left, aren't they?" I asked.

"How did you know?"

"An impression. They're nearly 12,000 feet."

"Do they fill you with ambition, Baby-face?"

"A bit."

The West Face . . . The North Face . . . Lochmatter—Leininger—Bonatti—Magnone . . . I like the sound of the names of those great climbers.

"Are the Petites-Charmoz very difficult?" I asked.

"No."

"Would I be able to manage them?"

"Perhaps. Why?"

I did not answer.

I had never known Piraly to be so silent as he was that day on the Mer de Glace. He seemed to be worried. And then he turned to Maurice and said the same thing about me.

"I don't like it when Colette doesn't talk. There must be something wrong."

Another way of saying that I'm a chatterbox, which is certainly the case. But if I was not talking much just then it was because I wanted to husband my strength. I was going to need it.

And I was thinking of Rolande, Gilberte and Michele, who were at that moment on the Petites-Charmoz. They had been studying maps yesterday, and they made me run my finger over one that was in relief . . . Why is it that when we are preparing for a small excursion we are always allured by great peaks that are beyond our capacity? It is the names that sing in our ears and turn our holidays into song.

"This feels hollow, don't you think?"

"It's just the axes striking against stones and ice."

"Look out—there's a step." Piraly, whom I was now following, did not say whether the step was up or down; the movement of his rucksack told me. "One stride." This time it was a question of stepping over a narrow fissure. It is important not to confuse "step" with "stride"—which is precisely what I did . . .

"Watch it!"

"You said, a step!"

"No, I said a stride."

I was flat on my face with my right leg in the hole . . .

"Suppose we stop for a bit," said Maurice. "I could do with something to eat."

"We aren't likely to die of hunger, with all the stuff we're carrying! Colette doesn't believe in starving us."

"I only want to keep your strength up," I said. "And did anyone think of bringing a flask of tea?"

They looked blank. They had completely forgotten.

"I'm not used to high altitudes," I said. "I soon get dried up."

"We'll have a drink when we arrive."

We clambered on over interminable moraines with Piraly and Maurice taking it in turns to steer me through that labyrinth. I hung on to the rucksack in front of me and followed its movements, which we had found to be the most efficient method for me to adopt. I trusted to my sense of balance and the soles of my boots and, when I was tired, the shoulders of my companions. I was not always conscious of what this meant, but they were, and there were sardonic remarks about "our darling featherweight" . .

"If you weigh nine stone at 3000 feet you must obviously weigh double at 4500—and so on, in geometrical progression."

"It's a matter of great scientific interest," I said.

"We ought to keep records and study it with care."

"There's one place where one would be able to climb without any trouble at all," I said. "On the moon."

"I don't want to be the first to go there!"

"Well, that's a pity. I can just picture you, Maurice, exploring the Copernicus Crater or the Soviet Mountains, 40,000 feet!"

"That'd teach me not to forget the tea-flask, wouldn't it!"

My companions were watching out for the red-painted cairns which marked the path. The valley was far below us with our troubles and the problems of our daily lives. Here everything was purified, everything clear . . .

I did not feel a stranger among those moraines where we had been wandering for so many hours. I had a profound sense of being where destiny intended me to be. I was living intensely in the present, every minute and every second. The shifting, crumbling surface, with never a solid foothold, gradually absorbed all the best of my energies. Those huge piles of rock and rubble, which to the eye must seem immovable, to me conveyed a sensation of confused life, persistent and unexpected. Everything seemed to echo, stones rolled and slid, mud squelched more quietly . . . Those heaps were in every shape and form. Providence held them together, the same Providence that was now guiding our footsteps . . .

Only one thing mattered, to put my foot in the place where the leader's had been a moment before and conform to the rhythm. With Piraly it was easy; our strides matched; he needed only to give brief instructions and I felt safe. With Maurice it was different. His long legs made it hard for me to keep in step, and we tired each other in consequence. But no one could have been more patient and kind. He showered me with words of guidance!

A party overtook us. I had not even heard them coming. In my surprise I started a small avalanche of pebbles and there was loud laughter—"It's worse than the Cervin!"

Somebody once said jestingly to me: "You must give your guardian angel a lot of trouble!"

"I'm sure I do. But don't forget that's what he's for!"

In passing I noticed a rock studded with quartz crystals. Previous parties had tried to root them out with their axes. We did the same, and the small fragment we secured is still in my possession.

After an approach climb which called for all my concentration we reached the foot of the Egralets, and anyone who has been there will know what this meant. I felt that it was too much for me, despite the ladders and ramps, and I said to the guide, Lionel Terray, whom we passed, "I've run out of courage." He was one of the great mountaineers, now on his way back from the Aiguille du Jardin. He shook hands with us and wished us luck.

I must again pay tribute to the tireless devotion and extreme patience of my guide, Piraly, of Maurice and of another young guide who, if I remember rightly, said that he was the nephew of Louis Comte, of Chamonix.

We climbed slowly and in silence, with frequent pauses. Friends had warned me on another occasion: "If you find things aren't going well, don't worry. Try to keep your nerves under control and let yourself be steered. It may not be very heroic, but that can't be helped."

So I let myself be steered like the infant-mountaineer I am and always will be. Sometimes Maurice took hold of my foot and put it in the best place. The same thing happened to a friend of mine on the Aiguille du Gouter.

We came to Talèfre, the Garden of Talèfre, the most beautiful bowl in the world; and Maurice at once started taking photographs, his favourite pastime.

We sat on the scented grass, brushed by the wind, and I marvelled to hear my companions exclaim in rapture at the beauty of the sunset. Used to the mountains though they were, they never ceased to rejoice in them or in the wonders of Nature.

But how could one fail to be moved? Such joys are inexhaustible. Whoever we may be, it is beauty that we contemplate, with our poor human means. Beauty and stillness, the stillness in which music rises, in which symphonies are born—in which, at times, we hear the voice of God. And as a background the deep note of rushing waters below us. I wish I could imprint it on my memory so that it would be with me all my life, the song of the rapids of Talèfre.

"It's wonderful!" cried Maurice. "Wait a minute, Piraly, I'm going to take another photograph. We've got time. Those snowy peaks and needles gleaming in the sun and going out one after another—le Triolet, la Ravanel-Mummery, La Verte, le Moine and the rest of them . . . They're still alight, while the Grandes-Jorasses are already in shadow; and down below the glaciers look dingy and dark . . ."

Dusk was falling and we moved on to the Refuge du Couvercle —the Couvercle shelter. I touched the small plants I had put in my pocket, hoping to be able to plant them in the garden at home.

"What is the Aiguille Verte, the Green Needle, like?" I asked Piraly. "I've read about it so often in books on mountaineering. I never thought I should be so near it."

"It's a difficult mountain with four ridges running roughly to all four points of the compass, and four complicated faces."

"Maurice," I said, "do you believe that Croz, Mummery and Cordier were really heroes?"

"Yes, all the pathfinders were heroes, because any climb is more difficult for the man who first attempts it. There's always the element of the unknown, the mystery which is part of its attraction. Their technique wasn't as highly-developed as ours. They took their lives in their hands and won, and no one can rob them of their victory. They are models for us all, and that is why we hold them in veneration."

"It's splendid, and wonderfully uplifting."

I quenched my thirst at a stream. We had been on the move for six and a half hours, and it had cost me a great effort.

"That'll do," said Piraly. "What a child you are! You'll get something better to drink at the shelter."

"I love the mountain water."

There were a few rocks to be negotiated, there was snow, and then I heard the noise of the engine driving the generator which lights the shelter. We were there!

The big, brightly-lighted general-room, and the noise that was going on in it, caused me to feel a little dazed after the silence outside. I did not know if I was happy or not; the mountains are not easy, they are no joke. I tried to relax.

As always when I had perspired a great deal I sipped slightly saline water to replace the salt that I had sweated out of my system and that is so necessary to sustain strength and nervous tension. We were the last to arrive, and by the time we had eaten a substantial meal it was time for bed. Most of the lights were out and everything was quiet. But before going up to the dormitory we went out to the terrace.

The silence . . . That paradise was bathed in moonlight, and a thought rose in my mind—"Oh, moon that I love so much, soft distant light that I saw over the plain when as a child I came in from the garden with father, mirrored in pale water—tonight I see you again, the friend upon my path . . ."

My two companions, who as a rule joked and laughed so loudly, were also in a meditative mood.

"Do you see that star, Piraly, to the left of the Grandes-Jorasses?" asked Maurice.

"There are stars everywhere. It's a wonderful night."

"And what do the mountains look like?" I asked.

"You see their shadow, and their huge silhouettes outlined against the sky. They're not all lighted up in the same way. The mass of the Grandes-Jorasses is darker."

"It must be very impressive."

"It's beautiful."

This was one of the few times in my life when I intensely longed to be able to see with my eyes, but I said nothing about it to my companions. There had been another such moment on the summit of the Tondu a year ago, in broad daylight . . . The Grandes-Jorasses, that noble northern wall, so alluring, so much desired and so cruel, which occupies nearly a mile of the horizon with its five peaks, Young, Margarita, Michel-Croz, Whymper, Walker . . . That vast creation of rock and ice with its fissures, its dihedrals, its overhanging crags, would one day subside and be flattened—the geologists knew it. But while it still exists—for millions of years to come—its purpose is to inspire man with the sense of Beauty and Greatness.

At three in the morning (it was 23rd August, 1961) the shelter dormitory began to empty. Young men and women vanished with their torches. Where were they off to? Some, perhaps, to the Aiguille Verte; others, certainly, to the Aiguille du Moine, the Monk's Needle.

My companions were both still asleep, but I couldn't get to sleep again. I had entirely agreed last night when we had decided not to proceed with our original plan, but now I began to argue with myself. Last night I had been tired, but now I was not.

"But the original plan would probably be too much for you," I reasoned. "Surely it would be. You know what you were like yesterday."

"I wasn't the one who made the plan."

"And yet you aren't satisfied?"

"Yes, but I think it's a pity to have come so far and then just go down again."

"Well, Pink-cheeks," said Maurice. "There are some alpine choughs flying about outside. I think I'll film them."

It was clear that Maurice was no more anxious than I to go back to the valley. The weather was fine and I felt thoroughly rested.

"Monsieur Piraly," I said firmly, "can't we go on?"

"We should have started sooner."

"But don't you think—?"

"We'll try the first few chimneys, if you like."

The day was perfect. We crossed the moraines of the Glacier du Moine, the Monk's Glacier, and put on crampons for the steep slope. Maurice filmed and took snapshots as usual.

"Everything O.K., Pink-cheeks?" he asked me.

"It's wonderful!"

"Colette," said Piraly, "I'm going first. Dig your crampons well in and I'll tell you when to move."

When I had come up with Piraly it was Maurice's turn, and so on.

I found suddenly that I was no longer scared on a loose rope. Although the ice surface was steep I went at it boldly. The hot sun had renewed my strength. The mountains are a wonderful school. I was sure now that it would have been wrong for me to leave the shelter without going higher.

"I can hear someone talking!" I exclaimed.

"Yes, there's a party on the Moine ridge, although we can't see them."

"It's extraordinary how sound carries. They might be a few yards away."

"I've had an idea," said Piraly. "We'll go up the Chien Rouge, over to our right. It's a modest target, but still it's something to aim at."

"All right. I don't mind missing the Aiguille and barking my shins in its chimneys. I wasn't so keen on that idea."

More loose-rope climbing up steep slopes. Today, more than ever, I found it thrilling. My crampons gripped well. I was able to walk upright instead of on all fours, as I had done last year on the Tondu. And then we came to rock and were able to take off the crampons, and I no longer needed to use my ice-axe.

That morning the rocks filled me with happiness and I felt wonderfully relaxed. This was strange, and I do not understand it. Or rather, I do—I always find happiness in activity, provided I'm not too strung-up.

"Are you enjoying yourself?"

"Very much. Is the Chien Rouge really like a dog?"

"Like a dog's head. The red rock's very pretty in the sunshine."

While Maurice amused himself with his cameras Piraly and I continued the ascent. He guided me with his voice, but I had to devise my own methods of following. I was in a state of perfect, euphoric happiness. Everything seemed easy, a thing that had never happened to me before, and I climbed without effort. Maurice took advantage of this to give me further instructions.

"Turn your face this way, love. Relax your arms a little, you're pressed too tight to the rock. Try it again."

We had reached our objective and I was sorry it was so soon over. Now we were climbing simply for the fun of it. I found holds without any trouble and was rather astonished at myself.

"Go on, Colette, but let me see your face," said Maurice, still intent on his photographs. "That's it. Now try and find a place for your right foot."

"I've only got a hold for my left. How difficult you are!"

"Wave to me with your right hand."

Piraly was above us, but he could go no further because there were no more holds. For my part, I was nicely balanced on my left foot with my hands resting on the rock-face; I felt perfectly comfortable.

I had noticed that Maurice chose to address me in the familiar second person singular when giving me orders, and I said laughing:

"I thought people only called each other 'tu' when they were over 12,000 feet?"

"That be blowed for a yarn. It doesn't matter how high you are."

"How high are we?"

"Not even 10,000."

"You make it sound as though it were nothing at all."

Maurice took endless photographs of Mont Blanc, the Grandes-Jorasses and the glaciers, and we kept up our joking all the way back to Chamonix, so that my head reeled. Piraly was moved to remark: "Well, it may not have been a tremendous climb in all respects, but we enjoyed ourselves like a pack of children and we laughed a lot."

It must be said that those high spirits were particularly helpful on the way down.

On the Moine glacier I was bombarded with snowballs because I preferred to glissade rather than walk upright, which always alarms me on a steep slope, particularly when one has to traverse. You can't beat sliding! The seat of my trousers was especially designed for it. That's the only way it ever gets worn out.

My companions were quite out of hand. We scrambled down the pebbly slope and got back to the Couvercle. The sun was high in the sky, but alas, we had to return to the valley. It cost me a pang to say goodbye to the keeper at the shelter.

"I'll be back!"

"Yesterday you thought the going was too hard."

"I know. But I hope that someday I shall have the luck to come again."

Maurice with a flourish wrote our names in the guest-book, and the date; and with an eye on me he added something like, "Piraly went on ahead to fix up a few pre-fabricated snow-slides to facilitate our descent . . ."

I hope that those coming after us, when they turn the pages of that old book and read those words, written on 23rd August, 1961, will understand something of our happiness and triumph, despite our difficulties.

The descent was arduous, although the Leschaux glacier enabled us to avoid a good many moraines. When we arrived at Montenvers we ran into a Swiss guide from Valais whom we had met in the shelter. He said to me simply: "My respects, Mademoiselle. The Couvercle is not as easy as all that."

6

Mont Blanc du Tacul

ON 27th August we decided that the next day we would go to the Tacul.

"A very nice snow climb, a good 13,000 feet," said Piraly.

"How does it compare with other climbs?"

"It's very different from anything we've done so far, but you'll enjoy it, I'm sure."

The 28th promised to be magnificently fine. The air on the summit of the Aiguille du Midi had a wonderfully keen, fresh smell. It was early.

We had put sealing-material on our boots to stop the snow getting in. We made the descent of the ridge, and I found Maurice more enterprising than Raymond had been the year before. He was already busy with his camera.

We reached the Col du Midi without trouble and started up the slope of the Tacul. Maurice led, and it pleased him every so and so often to make us stand shivering while he put in a new film.

"You might at least choose somewhere sunny!"

"I'm ready now. Onward—to the heights!"

And off he would go with giant strides as though he were walking along the streets of Chamonix. He kept it up even when the slope grew really steep, until I was completely out of breath.

Then we stopped playing the fool and Piraly took the lead. We fell into a very much slower pace, one to which I was quite unused and to which at first I had difficulty in adapting myself. We were all silent as we gradually gained height. It was going to be a hard climb, but I was delighted. I was in good condition, the snow suited me and I was sure that all would be well. The stiffness in my legs wore off and I began to get the rhythm.

My companions were gazing at the Cervin, which in the clear

At the climbing-school at Saint-Gervais

With Louis Piraly on the Aiguille du Midi

morning air looked as though it were quite close. I pictured that view, the Cervin, the Matterhorn, 15,000 feet, that great pyramid with its four ridges, Zmutt, Hoernli, Lion and Furgen . . . I thought of the great names in its history, Whymper and the tragic rope-party in 1865 when Michel Croz was killed; Jean-Antoine Carrel, and many others since . . .

The ascent became very steep. We checked our rope with great care and moved upward one at a time. Needless to say, we were all wearing crampons, so there was no problem where our feet were concerned. The sun was dazzling. There was a void on our right, I knew it, I could feel it because the air on that side was very cold. But I felt no fear at all. I was at the top of my form and full of confidence as I climbed on my own, some distance behind Piraly, who by now knew me well enough to guess my frame of mind.

"Things are going well today, Colette."

"Yes, wonderfully well. This is a bit like the Moine glacier, but longer."

"I said you'd enjoy it, didn't I?"

The crampons were gripping well. There were good footholds, but all the same I used my hands for greater safety, because it was so steep. My eyes were at my fingertips.

"Maurice," I said, without turning, "am I keeping to the track?"

"You're doing fine. Carry on."

The slope became less steep and we rested a little.

"It's good and firm," said Piraly. "We can go on. Colette, you're going to have to jump."

"How far?"

"About a yard."

"I'm not sure if I . . . ." I felt the other side of the crevasse with my ice-axe.

"Go to it, Baby-face," said Maurice. "Don't be coy!"

I loved everything about that climb, the setting, the healthy companionship. I could not have been more happy. My greatest joy is in action, in using my strength, in having something to do. This was hard and splendid labour. The three of us made a wonderful team. I had a great admiration for my companions and a sense of profound gratitude for the trouble they took for my sake. Their happiness lay in pleasing me. It must be said that I am not always full of smiles, but I was that morning; everything was perfect.

Tunes often run through my head when I am climbing. On Mont Tondu it had been Borodin—"On the Steppes of Central Asia". In the Vallée Blanche, on our way to the Col du Géant, I had been haunted by a piece by Grieg which I had played at a school concert as one half of a piano duet. And among the moraines of the Mer de Glace it had been a melody from Beethoven's violin concerto.

The music that flooded through my mind that morning, one of the most perfect of my life, came to me from what seemed to be the very distant past. I had played it on the piano eleven years ago at the prize-giving concert at the Ecole de Saint-Mandé. (I gained a distinction and left that school for the Insitution Nationale.) It was Saint-Saëns' "Chant du Gygne."

Why should I have thought of the dying swan on that particular morning? No doubt because its whiteness and purity so perfectly matched the brilliant light of the sky and snow, and also because its rhythm was attuned to our climb. I could not get it out of my head. Yet it was sad and the day was filled with happiness. So I livened it up a little, half against my will, and I hope Saint-Saëns will forgive me.

We passed below seracs, formidable walls of ice a hundred feet high. I could feel them on our left, like an overhanging screen. One was a good deal melted at its base—a place where it would be unwise to linger later on, when the sun was at full strength.

We continued to climb, and now I was beginning to feel tired. I had to be doubly careful.

"Keep well in to your left," said Piraly. "Have you got a good foothold?"

"Yes."

"Well, don't move. I'll go ahead to secure you. I'll tell you when to come."

The classic phrase. Piraly stopped higher up, but I waited in vain for his signal. What was happening? A few yards behind me Maurice was also motionless, awaiting his turn like me, and I wondered what he was thinking. I was tempted to ask, but the words died on my lips. There were too many words, too many thoughts suspended in that silence for me to disturb them.

"My children, I'm afraid we shall have to turn back."

Neither Maurice nor I said anything. We waited to be told more. The silence was solemn, and I thought, "Please let us go on!—well, do what you think best! . . ."

To me it was as though for a few seconds, or minutes, time had come to a stop; and this feeling was later confirmed by Piraly, who said to me when we were back in the valley, "You know, I hesitated for a long time. I said to myself, 'I must have the strength of mind to turn back'."

We were on a narrow shelf with a steep drop on our right. Supporting myself on my ice-axe, with my crampons dug well in, I touched the ice-wall with my left hand and waited. While the silence lasted there was always hope.

"Maurice, I don't like it," said Piraly.

"Surely we can get Colette up between us?"

"Yes, but what about the descent? There's an overhang. If she misses her footing she'll be hanging by her ice-axe and it might break, in which case we'd all drop about 6000 feet into the Grands-Mulets. If I was told that there was an injured person up above who needed rescuing I'd go on, even with Colette. But it's only our own lives we're playing with, and we've no right to risk them unnecessarily."

We had to accept his decision, which reflected all the wisdom and prudence of an expert mountaineer. To say that I did so light-heartedly and with a smile would be rather far from the truth. I simply made myself as impassive as the ice which barred our way, which was the best I could do. It is very hard to have to turn back after hours of effort. To abandon a climb calls for far more strength of mind than to go on with it.

"Cheer up, Baby-face," said Maurice. "There are plenty of people with eyes who couldn't have done half as well as you have. We're at about 13,000 feet. The Aiguille du Midi is below us."

"Have you a flask of tea?"

"We've got two," said Piraly. "We might find a corner to sit down and have something to eat."

"All right."

Before leaving that spot I inscribed in fancy a line from *Cyrano de Bergérac* in the snow—"And it is all the more splendid when it is in vain." We threw a few snowballs to restore our spirits.

"You'd better save your energy, love," said Maurice. "We've got to get back to Chamonix."

"I don't want to go down. I like it up here in the twelve-thousands."

I stroked my ice-axe, as I often did—its blade was beautiful and smooth, with polished surfaces—while my companions contemplated the terrible abyss below us, which caused us no alarm because we were taking every possible precaution.

Because I can't see where I'm putting my feet I prefer to make an awkward descent a step at a time, sitting on the snow. It is less elegant but far safer. It is easy enough to follow a track with one's hands when one is going up, but I defy anyone to follow a track going down with their eyes closed, and it isn't easy to go on all fours with one's head lower than one's behind. For a sightless person my method is certainly the best.

When the slope became less steep I slid on my behind. Luckily I was still roped, because I'm not very good at braking with my ice-axe and I came in for some severe scoldings!

We were overtaken by another guide, Frison-Roche, and his client on their way down from the summit.

"You were quite right not to go any further," he said. "There's a party of Italians up there who are having a job to get down."

My companions watched the Italians for a long time.

"They aren't very sure of themselves."

"They're scared of the drop. They're coming down on their bottoms, like Colette, a yard at a time."

"Providing they don't start slipping."

"Yes. The snow's soft under this burning sun!"

"I'm thankful we didn't go any further," I said.

We went back by way of the Col du Midi and overtook Monsieur Frison-Roche at the bottom of the ridge. While Maurice took a photograph the two guides discussed films that might be made for television documentaries. I was delighted to have met Frison-Roche amid those splendid mountains. He has written a number of books. I wondered if he realised that they have been transcribed in braille, and that I had read them, like everyone else.

And then we had to climb back up the Midi-Plan ridge—a big effort, particularly when one lacks the satisfaction of having done what one set out to do. What robbed me of my breath was not so much the altitude as the steepness of the ascent. My ears sang a little, and I had to stop and rest quite often, and I drank the last of our tea. The heat of the sun was almost unbearable, despite the very cool breeze blowing at that altitude—the two separate elements do not cancel out but seem rather to add to each other. My head was unprotected, but I made myself a passable hat out of a white hand-kerchief and some boot laces.

We passed an English pair who were making the descent of the ridge without being roped, which was very rash. We persuaded them of this.

Maurice was busy with his film camera, insatiable as ever. Every now and then he gave me a little prod with his ice-axe to keep me in line.

We waved to the sightseers passing above our heads in cable-cars. There was to be a tragedy on that line the very next day. A jet-plane cut through the supporting cable; several cars fell into the abyss and a number of passengers were killed.

I found that climb very hard. I was gasping for breath and the sun was awful, although the feeling of empty space on either side of us was sublime. I deliberately tried to picture it to see what my reaction would be in my present state of fatigue.

But I was too tired to feel afraid. It is strange how one's reactions vary with every climb. My companions did everything they could to help me, using calmness and patience and stern words and jokes —anything to keep up my morale!

"Pull yourself together, Baby-face! . . . You just haven't got the guts! We shall never make you into a real mountaineer . . . Cheer up! This is the last bend."

There were masses of people on the summit of the Aiguille du Midi. We made a halt at the Plan de l'Aiguille and refreshed our-selves with strawberry-syrup. I had discovered already that before plunging down 10,000 feet in half an hour by cable-car a short rest did me a lot of good; and anyway the people on the Plan were charming.

Back in Chamonix we went to the Choucas café for another strawberry-syrup. Apparently it is the place where mountaineers forgather, and it is most pleasant.

We had had a good day and were pleased with ourselves. But for me the details, varying according to circumstance, mattered far less than the fact that I had breathed the air of over 12,000 feet. That was something that I should never—never in my whole life!— forget.

7

The Col Infranchissable

I HAD spent a week beside the sea, but I was longing for the mountains, in particular for the Massif du Mont Blanc. So when I arrived at Saint-Gervais the first thing I did was to set about organising a nice little programme of climbs.

My first objective was the Col Infranchissable—the Unassailable Pass—which is about 11,000 feet.

On 9th August we climbed by way of the familiar, narrow path to spend the night at the Tré-La-Tête shelter. The weather was even better than it had been two years before, when we climbed the Mont Tondu. Piraly was with me and the Abbé Meynet, who had come with us on that earlier climb, was also able to join us. As always, he was the best of team-mates.

"I'm not at all in training," I warned him. "I've only been four days in the mountains, and I've only done one little climb at 6000 to stretch my legs."

"Never mind. If it rains tomorrow you'll be able to rest at the Shelter."

"Don't talk to me about rain! Last year we planned three times to do the Infranchissable and the weather prevented us every time."

"I'm sure it'll be fine tomorrow."

I devoured my cold meal at the shelter, washed down with soup and numerous cups of tea. I was happy to meet Madame Paul Dujon of Saint-Gervais, who told me that my two friends who set out for the Bérangère today had had a good climb. Before turning in we went on to the terrace, as we always did. The evening was beautiful, cool and still.

"The sky's red, Piraly," said Meynet. "Is that a good sign?"

"Yes, it should mean a perfect day tomorrow."

"When we were at Versailles," I said, "my father always told me that a red sky at night meant wind and rain in the morning."

"Not in these parts. It's a beautiful sky, but it'll only last a few minutes. Mont Joly is over on our left, with Les Miages in front of it; and further away, to the right, there's the Col des Glaciers, the Aiguille des Glaciers and the Lanchettes."

"It's so wonderfully peaceful," said Meynet.

"Can you see the Tondu?" I asked.

"No, it's in darkness already."

"Where exactly are we going tomorrow, to the Infranchissable or the Bérangère? There's only a few hundred feet difference in height."

"We'll see when the time comes. We'd better turn in. We shall have to be up at three!"

"Well, mind you wake up!" I said to my companions.

I shared the dormitory with some young people who were going to cross the Miages. It was very comfortable but I did not get to sleep for some time. Late-comers were moving about in the dining-room over our heads.

Would I climb well tomorrow? I had persuaded Meynet to put himself out on my account, and I did not want to let him down. Would it be left to me to decide whether we should attempt the Bérangère or the Infranchissable? The first was the steeper climb, but shorter. Well, we should have to see, as Piraly said, and meanwhile I must get some sleep . . . I love those nights in the shelters.

At three o'clock on the morning of 10th August the shelter was teeming with activity. I went up to the dining-room to get a cup of tea and found my companions there already.

"I'm furious," I said. "I've just broken the dark glasses I bought last week. A fine beginning!"

Before leaving the shelter we took everything possible out of our rucksacks so as only to have to carry essentials.

It was cold and the sky was brilliant with stars. We were one of the first parties to leave and I was glad of that. People called out, wishing us a good climb; and then we were in the midst of silence—nothing to be heard but the sound of falling water in the darkness. If someone were to offer me a million pounds to give up mountain climbing I would not accept. There are things that cannot be reckoned or paid for in money. Night-time in the mountains is a living thing that makes a lasting impression on the heart, something that cannot be grasped when one is down in the valley of men.

"Well," asked Meynet, "which is it to be, the Bérangère or the 'Infran'?"

"I don't know," I said. "I've been dreaming of the Bérangère for a long time, but Piraly doesn't much care for that one."

"But haven't you ever dreamed of the Infranchissable?"

"Of course. I'd like to do both, one today and one tomorrow. Would that be impossible?"

"We'll make up our minds when we reach the Tré-La-Grande hut," said Piraly. "That's where the paths separate. So we've two and a half hours to get into our stride."

We negotiated the moraines leading to the Tré-La-Tête glacier with me in the middle and Meynet behind. We had to cross a number of small streams. Another party came up behind us and we went on together.

"Where are you making for?"

"The Tondu. Is it difficult?"

"Not very. We did it two years ago."

I was letting myself be distracted by the newcomers' talk, and Piraly disapproved, because it made me less careful in placing my feet. They were joking among themselves.

"What did we ever do to the good God for him to pile all these heaps of stones in our way?"

There was general laughter, and I slipped and fell.

"Do you want a torch?"

"No thanks. I can manage."

I hung on to Piraly's rucksack and got along comfortably—so much so, indeed, that the strangers behind us did not realise my disability. The moraines seemed longer than ever this year, but at length we reached the glacier.

My nice glacier. I was happy to be there again because I have a special fondness for it. I recalled 19th August, 1961, when we had intended to climb it, but my guide had been unwell and could not leave the shelter. It had been a starry night, like now, and I had been very sad at having to go back to the valley without having even set foot on the ice.

The glacier was dirty, covered with debris. We followed a zig-zag path and traversed to the right to get on to the moraine. The other party separated from us, and now there was complete silence. We got along fast, and I was in fine form, stimulated by the cold.

Then we followed the fresh ice at the centre of the glacier, our soles gripping well. I was still holding Piraly's rucksack and we had no trouble. We were not yet roped, and made excellent progress.

Melt-water welled up here, forming small whirlpools and streams which flowed into the larger stream lower down. The day was dawning and, in the words of the chamois-hunters' song, "The mountains were singing".

"I like this better than the Mer de Glace," I said.

"It's exactly the same. You don't remember much about your previous climbs."

"I remember perfectly. What tired me so much on the Mer de Glace were all the ridges, like solid waves. They formed a series of crests and hollows which I couldn't see. Here it's quite steep, I know, but the surface is less billowy and I find it easier."

We moved over to the left, where the surface was better still, and then, after negotiating some moraines, came back to the middle. We passed a party on their way to the Miages, a little to our right. Now and then Piraly had to cut footholds for me. Bare ice was followed by patches of shingle and then a mixture of the two—chaotic but good. For two hours we continued to ascend that wonderful glacier, veering now to the left, now back to the centre to avoid seracs and find paths which were easier for me. We were in high spirits. There were a number of parties behind us.

After leaving the path to the Tondu on our right we embarked on the endless series of *névés*, stretches of frozen snow, that led to Tré-La-Grande. Meynet, who had hitherto been very quiet, told us about his climbing adventures last year—assaulting the Aiguille du Tour, and being held up and having to bivouac for the night at the foot of the Egralets, and so on. He made a very funny story of it and I laughed a lot. He's a wonderful companion. We were roped by now, and I was beginning to find the glacier monotonous and the névés very trying.

"This is only the beginning," said Piraly. "The glacier's five miles long, without counting the detours we shall have to make. The Infranchissable is right at the top."

"Well, we shall have to do it in stages. Is the hut very far off?"

"About half an hour. It's over there, on the rocks. We shall see it soon."

I prefer bare ice. These rather steep névés were slowing us up, and the surface was bound to get softer, particularly when the sun came out. Finally we reached the rocks and the sound of running water, which pleased me, not because I was thirsty but because I love the sound of water, which soothes and relaxes me. I remembered that this time I had a flask of tea in my rucksack, all for myself. It was a wonderful thought after my agonies last year on the Chien Rouge and the Tacul.

"Well, where's the hut?"

"We're there."

Two other men reached it just as we did. They were very friendly. We asked where they were going.

"We haven't decided. We thought of the Miages, but it's a bit late, isn't it? We'll make up our minds when we reach the Col. And where are you heading for?"

"For the Infranchissable." I said. "It's a longer climb but not so steep. I'm not in very good training and Abbé Meynet prefers it anyway, so it suits us all."

I planted my ice-axe in the snow and sat down to have a drink and munch a few lumps of sugar. But my axe did not hold. I banged it in again, nearer my foot—too near!—and uttered a yelp.

"Oh! I've hurt myself. I've buried my ice-axe in my boot."

"You're joking," said Meynet.

"No, really, I've hurt myself."

"But you aren't strong enough to have cut through your boot."

"I'm not so sure."

Piraly was talking to the two strangers. I sat down and began to take off my boot. It was idiotic—to go and injure oneself when one was resting! I was furious; I had never done anything of the kind before. The axe had cut through the double tongue of my boot, the thick outer stocking, the sock and the foot strapping, and had slightly cut my foot, badly enough to make it bleed. Meynet had to believe me now. I pulled off the strapping and dabbed on mercuro-chrome from the small tube I always carry in the pocket of my anorak. One of the strangers gave me surgical spirit and gauze. All was well.

After I had dressed my wound and refreshed myself we set out again. But as we got higher my progress became slower. The sun was beginning to blaze, which was disastrous for me.

"We both like the sun," my companions said.

"So do I, but not when I'm making an ascent. It's so tiring. I'd sooner there were clouds."

"She's a difficult girl, isn't she? She wants everything made to measure, the mountains, the sky and the time-table!"

The two other men had now got a long way ahead of us. I no longer even tried to keep a steady rhythm. The snow had become terribly soft; the drifts were monotonous and I could never guess when they would end. We made an ascending traverse with the slope on our right. Apparently it was not really very formidable, but still it worried me and I put on my crampons to give myself a greater sense of security. After that I went slower than ever, feeling the irons heavy on my feet.

Piraly described the mountains and told me their names— Aiguille des Glaciers, Col de la Scie, Glacier de la Lex-Blanche and the Aiguille de la Lex-Blanche, of evil celebrity in our district of the Contamines because of two accidents in recent years which had cost the lives of six people.

Over on the other side was Italy, and there were the Col de Tré-La-Tête, l'Aiguille Centrale, l'Aiguille Blanche de Tré-La-Tête and the Tête Carrée, the highest of all, to the right of the Col Infranchissable.

We were now at an altitude of 10,000 feet. The air was cold, but the sun burningly hot. I smeared my face with cream and took off my anorak and tied it round my waist. The pause while I did so gave me a chance to get my breath. We were well behind schedule. After getting along so well in the early hours I was now beginning to feel exhausted, perhaps from lack of training and because of the altitude, and perhaps also because the small injury to my foot had weakened me. I don't really know why it was, but I do know that my companions were very patient.

"You climbed much better on the Tondu, two years ago," said Meynet, "and it was the first real climb you had done."

"I'm sure I didn't," I retorted sharply. "That was much more difficult. I remember it vividly."

"We never seem to agree about anything."

"Why don't you just leave me here, in a safe place? I'll wait for you and promise not to move, and you can go on up to the top."

"Come, come, you can't give up as easily as that! We shall be there in an hour."

"Do you mean *really* an hour, or roughly an hour?"

"It's no good asking questions. Just keep going."

The snow here was like waves, and the slope was still on our right. I tried to place my feet correctly in those ups and downs that caught me round the calves and knees, but it was very tiring and I often had to stop. I again suggested that the others should go on without me, but they took no notice. If only the sun had been less hot! If only there had been a few clouds! I was sweating hard and feeling exhausted and I wanted to sit down. Meynet was against this because it broke the rhythm and wasted time and only increased the fatigue. I knew he was right but every hundred yards or so I had to pause because my heart was thumping so hard—a hundred and twenty to the minute, or more. It was idiotic, and it had never happened to me before. I wanted to give up, I felt sure I could never make it. I was no good for anything. I couldn't think what had happened to me this year.

I decided that I would give up climbing altogether, it was simply too difficult for a person without eyes. Never again to be in the high mountains—the thought made me more miserable than ever! Because at the same time I loved that mountain; no one will ever understand or know how much I loved it. I felt tears welling in my eyes, but I was determined not to break down and cry, because I knew that if I did it would be the end and I should go no further. So that proved that I still had a little willpower left. I sat down on the snow with Meynet on my right. He was quite calm. He knew, as we all did, that we must push on as fast as possible so as to be able to make the descent before the sun grew too hot, to avoid the risk of avalanches.

Piraly climbed a little higher, saying that he was looking for rock-crystals. He was very sweet. He gave me a chance to rest without making it too obvious that he was simply waiting for me. I heard him tapping with his ice-axe somewhere above us. The snowy slope stretched ahead of us and the sun blazed down. Everything was peaceful, and everything seemed to be waiting. No one hurried me. The very mountain seemed gentle, and more than ever I felt the force of its personality, as though it were a living thing.

"You must be brave, Colette," said Piraly. "Only twenty minutes more. Look out, here's another crevasse. We've jumped a good many, but this one's wider. Put your foot beside mine, measure the distance with your axe, and then jump."

"No, it's too wide! This time I simply can't!"

"Now, don't make me scold you! Who's in charge here?"

"But suppose I fall in?"

"Well, what's the rope for?"

I took a deep breath and made a perfect landing. But now, as we approached the Col, there was a whole network of crevasses, as though God had deliberately collected them to put them in my way Still, when all was said, I would sooner jump crevasses or cross them by snow-bridges than plough my way through endless névés. This at least was action. I had a sense of doing something worthwhile, real mountaineering. It was perhaps a hare-brained reaction, but no matter. Mine is not a sluggish temperament.

"Well, what about that Col? You said only twenty minutes."

"We're there! We've got the Tête Carrée on our right, and on our left is the Col des Miages, which those chaps we met at Tré-La-Grande should have reached by now. If we go a little further we shall have a magnificent view."

We're there! . . . The words filled me with delight. Eleven thousand feet. A wonderful climb! My last!

With eyesight you can see the summit, the goal; you know you're going to reach it, and with that stimulus you do reach it. But if you can't see you have to imagine the summit, and it's always a long way off, farther than you thought, too far. It calls for courage. I repeat in all humility: it calls for great courage.

I spread my anorak on the snow and sat down facing the sun, with the good north wind from the Col blowing on my back. We ate biscuits, chocolate, nougat and cheese, and I drank tea.

"You ought to go on to the other side," I said to my companions, "and see that magnificent view."

"All right, we'll unrope you. But understand, you're not to move. You're only a yard away from a big crevasse. You must stay sitting just where you are."

"I promise."

The two men went off, and at last I was alone, absolutely alone for half an hour! It had never happened to me before. To be alone at a height of 10,000 feet. The silence! There was only the sun and the cold wind and an occasional small fall of stones on my left, coming from the Tête Carrée.

I sat there listening with my whole being, and with my whole strength contemplating that mountain that I so dearly love. I contemplated it with an inward gaze, that of my soul; but I am sure that I could see all those mountains. I saw them and I thought, "This is my last climb, it's too difficult." I had managed to get here, but at the cost of great trouble to my companions. So much kindness. I thought of my parents, my brothers and my sister; I repeated the names of my nieces, my nephew and my dearest friends. Then I was silent, invoking in myself the great inward silence, that in which one is in contact with God the Creator. Was there anyone in the world, at that moment, as happy as I?

For the silence was not emptiness. The silence was Life, making one with the Word. That region was filled with silence—that is to say, filled with life. The mountains did not frighten me, or the crevasses either. If God had allowed me to come here it was because it was my place; it was for a reason, and the reason was the message that one day I would give to the world. But I could not believe that I would ever come here again.

All those people whose senses are benumbed by noise should come to this place, although all cannot do so. Here one is truly alive. I knew that if I gave up the mountains altogether I should not be able to go on living, I love them too much.

I no longer wanted to think, and stopped thinking; I heard the sound of a distant aeroplane . . . The minutes slipped by. I was not wearing my watch, I had no notion of time; but it was better so, the utter abandonment of body and mind . . . I was perfectly and wonderfully alone for a little while. My two companions would never know my happiness, or the great kindness they had done me in staying away so long. They were looking at the view—the Italian Glacier de Miage and the Bionnassay, and beyond these the Aiguille de Bionnassay, the Dôme du Gouter and Mont Blanc, so near that one might tough it with one's finger. At that moment I did not envy them. My contemplation of the mountains was a thousand times more wonderful, and I believe that even to say this is to say too little . . .

At length they returned to me.

"I hope we haven't kept you waiting too long."

"Oh, no, you should have stayed longer."

"We've got to get back. It's a quarter to twelve. Just one or two photos and then we must be off."

We had to cross the crevasses again, and I had to be talked into jumping the wide one, but again I managed it. The snow was getting terribly soft and my crampons bothered me. Meynet was rather cross when he found that the descent was taking as long as the ascent had done.

I took off my irons and held on to Piraly's rucksack and we went faster, our first objective being the hut at Tré-La-Grande. I kept slipping and was scolded for it. I did my best to be careful and place my feet properly, but I found it terribly hard work. I must have been very tired.

I fell again, carrying Piraly with me and he checked our slide with his axe. Fortunately the slope was not too steep at that point, but this earned me a severe lecture, although I was up on my feet again in less time that it takes to write. So then I tried harder than ever, feeling that we should never reach that wretched hut.

Sometimes I simply followed the rope, and sometimes I hung on to Piraly. We were getting along dreadfully slowly, although Meynet did not seem to mind. At last, after we had worked our way down a second snow slope, the hut came in sight. I promptly slipped again and Piraly fell on top of me and nearly put his boot in my face.

"Will you for God's sake dig your heels in!" he demanded furiously, jerking me to my feet. "It isn't much to ask!"

I felt tears running down my cheeks, and Meynet completed my distress by saying: "It's no use getting worked up about it. The thing is to discover whether you're capable of serious climbing."

I did not answer. Of course they were right. They, too, were tired, and they'd had such a hard time with me and for so little reward. I felt sorry for them both. I followed Piraly without saying a word, taking great care to place my feet in his tracks so as not to slip—and, Heaven knows how, I slipped all the same! . . .

After leaving the hut, where quite a number of people were sunbathing, I slid down most of the snow slopes, mostly on my behind, which is a thing I love doing although this time I found it as exhausting as everything else . . . Moraines, rocks, snowdrifts, bare ice, and the sun and my companions hurrying me along—

it took us several hours to get back to the shelter at Tré-La-Tête.

I was utterly worn out but happy—difficult though the climb had been, and even though it might be my last, I did not regret it. Laughing, I reminded Meynet of something he had said two years before—"The mountains are wonderful on the way down!" He no longer thought this and neither did I, so at last there was something we could agree about . . . We should not be attempting La Bérangère tomorrow. That tall, chaste lady would have to await another day.

8

Ice-Climb

ON 14th August, a morning splashed with sunshine, I went with Piraly to the Nid d'Aigle, a height of about 10,000 feet. We took the TMB (Tramway du Mont Blanc) from Saint-Gervais, a very pleasant and restful little cable-train from which one has wonderful views of the valleys of Montjoie and Chamonix with their beloved mountains, the ones with gentle slopes and the giants which fill me with wonderment and haunt my memory.

There were a great many noisy and happy holiday-makers at the Nid d'Aigle, the Eagle's Nest, some of whom were spending the day there while others were going on to the Tête Rousse, the Redhead, following the narrow, stony track, which is easy if one is well-shod.

Piraly led me along another path through the moraines which would bring us in twenty minutes to the Bionnassay glacier. We walked in silence, our ice-axes clicking rhythmically against the stones, both of us happy to be back on the heights. Piraly described the magical landscape through which we were passing and once again I was struck by his love of the mountains and his profound knowledge of them. I was deeply grateful to him for bringing me to this region, which is almost inaccessible to anyone who cannot see.

Ahead of us was the splendid northern face of the Aiguille de Bionnassay, reaching a height of nearly 13,000 feet. This face is so dangerous that it is better climbed at night, to avoid rock-falls. Piraly described it to me in detail, explaining its structure. He also talked about the Aiguille de Tricot and the Aiguille Earnest-Chapelland, both over 10,000 feet, the latter named after a famous guide from Saint-Gervais who met his death in the mountains. There was also the Arête de Tricot (the Tricot ridge), the Aiguille Inférieure de Tricot and the Col (the pass, or "neck") de Tricot, and beyond these the charming Vorassay range, coloured bright green in contrast to the white of the eternal snows.

The sky was almost cloudless, the air wonderfully keen. Above us was the new shelter on the Aiguille du Gouter, its aluminium shutters gleaming in the sunshine. It had only just been completed and was very comfortable, capable of accommodating over a hundred and fifty climbers, who rested there before embarking on the grand assault of Mont Blanc. We thought about this, I especially, but that year Mont Blanc was not for me.

Where the path was narrow, with small turns, Piraly let me find my way on my own, while keeping a sharp eye on me. I had absolute faith in him. We had come to know each other very well.

"Can you hear the party behind us?" he asked suddenly.

"Yes. Are they going to the glacier?"

"I rather think they're making for the Tête Rousse and have missed the path." Piraly shouted to them: "Hey, where are you heading for?"

"The Aiguille du Gouter."

"You've left it a bit late," said Piraly. "Do you know the best way to the Tête Rousse? It's steeper this way."

"Oh, we'll manage."

"Well, watch out for stones in the grand corridor. A girl was injured there this morning."

We let them pass us. They had no guide and were very sure of themselves. It is over-confidence of this kind that leads to rescue-operations. Piraly stood rather glumly watching them, and then we continued on our way to the glacier.

We met another party of exceedingly nice young people who were also making for the new shelter, where they intended to spend the night. They asked our advice about the best way of getting through the grand corridor of the Aiguille, which is extremely dangerous because of the frequent falls of loose rock. We wished them luck—our own objective was far more modest.

After crossing a small stream we began to climb a névé. Piraly was determined to teach me how to come down these slopes properly "en ramasse"—that is to say, to glissade down using the soles of one's boots like skis and braking with the ice-axe, which one holds in both hands. He stood at the bottom of the slope and I slid down to him. The first time I lost my footing and fell, which was what always happened. I had never learnt to brake properly or to keep my balance. But then I tried again and began to get the hang of it. I was not in the least afraid with Piraly there. We crossed a few moraines and repeated the exercise higher up. It was great fun.

Then the slope grew steeper. Piraly knew that what rather frightened me on a high climb was having to traverse a snow-slope, when one's feet are never on the same level. I was terrified of losing my grip altogether and going into an uncontrolled slide. To rid me of this quite unreasonable fear he made me make traverses alone, first with crampons and then without them, simply by planting my feet firmly and steadying myself with my ice-axe. And because we always worked so well together I now found it quite simple. Everything was still and silent, we were alone in that part of the glacier.

Presently we roped ourselves and I tried to learn more about crossing moraines, which I never like, although I must admit that after being on snow for a long time I rather enjoy the sensation of feeling something more solid, even if it is only loose stones, under my feet. It makes for variety, and although it is just as tiring the change has a relaxing effect.

Then, in the same methodical way, Piraly gave me a lesson in cutting footholds in the naked ice. Of course I would never be at the head of a rope-party, but it was essential for me to know at least the rudiments of the technique. Anyway I wanted to learn. I wanted to be as much as possible like other climbers. This was something that Piraly perfectly understood.

The first steps I cut were not very good, either too wide or too narrow. I held my axe wrongly and didn't hit hard enough and not in the same place. But then I began to get the knack. I examined the steps with my hand after cutting them, and when they improved I was very pleased with myself. I could stand in them, using irons, and I went on cutting until I had reached the top of the small wall of ice.

"What's beyond it?" I asked.

"A crevasse."

Piraly shouted down the crevasse so that I could judge its depth from the echo. Today it did not alarm me in the least and I leaned over it. I liked that glacier very much. I preferred it to the Mer de Glace, and, although I hardly dare say so, perhaps even to the Tré-La-Tête, although it was steeper and more dangerous than the latter, and very different in its conformation. I knew this because I had a relief-map of the whole Saint-Gervais sector back at the chalet. It was a tremendous help to me in forming a picture of mountains, valleys and glaciers, their heights and their slopes, and it also gave me some idea of perspective.

I cut footholds for a traverse, doing it reasonably well, and then was made to cut a series for a straight climb, which I found easier. All this delighted me. It was quite different from anything Piraly and I had hitherto done together. In the ordinary way I simply had to obey orders and move when and where I was told, however monotonous it might be; and long, thirsty hours under the sun, negotiating snow-slopes and moraines, can be very monotonous. But today I was playing an active part in the climb, with Piraly allowing me to move as I pleased. We were not pressed for time and no one was waiting for us in the valley. Indeed, I think the valley had almost ceased to exist where we were concerned.

We were at peace, and because I was not being prodded or made to hurry I moved more naturally and did everything more easily, without even being conscious of the fact. We jumped small crevasses, and here too there was running water. Its sound delighted my ears, but for once I was not thirsty. Just for fun I cut off a piece of ice and sucked it—and, of course, was told that I was an "urchin"!

We came to an awkward spot, and there was only one way of dealing with it. Piraly would have to lower me on the rope into a small crevasse. He would then follow me down, and we would climb up again a little further on, where it was easier.

"Quite a useful exercise," said Piraly. "If ever we find ourselves in real trouble you won't be scared at being let down on the end of a rope."

Well, certainly, being lowered at the end of a rope is very interesting, but I must confess that I prefer going down by myself on a secured rope. However, my opinion was not asked. Piraly climbed down beside me, cutting steps for himself, because there was no one up above to secure him. I was splashed with fragments of ice as he descended, which was chilly but not at all unpleasant.

A little further on I started cutting steps in a nice surface, and enjoyed doing so. But the wall was very sheer, and after I had cut five or six Piraly said: "I think we shall have to go further and try somewhere else."

"Don't you think we can manage to get out here?"

"It looks difficult to me. There's nothing to get hold of."

"Oh, but wait, there's a little crack on my right, about ten centimetres wide, and it goes on up! It's wonderful! Don't you think I could get up by jamming my hands and feet in it?"

"Yes, but it's too far over to your right, and you haven't cut steps for your feet so that you can reach it."

I thought for a moment and said: "I'm going to try. I think I can do it."

"All right, try if you like, but remember that I can't prevent you falling."

"There are some stones on the ice. Look out, I'm going to shift them."

Piraly stood below me, watching intently as I climbed and ready to catch me if I fell. But I knew I was not going to fall. I would not have exchanged that minute for all the riches in the world!

"Is my right foot all right. Because I've nowhere to put my left."

"Yes. I'll put my axe under your left foot. Go ahead. As soon as you've got a foot in the crack I'll put the axe under your other foot."

Piraly understood my reflexes better than anyone; it was the tenth or eleventh time we had been out together. He knew my movements and what I was thinking and what to say to me when I hesitated. He felt instinctively when I was afraid, but also knew when I was intoxicated by action—carried away by the game, as he said. And now I was in full flight, weighing my every move. I knew that I could not linger on those precarious holds, or on the axe which Piraly was holding at arm's length to support my foot. And he knew that in a matter of seconds I should have to change my holds and my position, and start climbing. He was calculating my moves just as I was doing. He waited in silence . . . And then I was in the little fissure in the ice which I had discovered.

"I'm up," I said simply. "Come on."

"So now I've got to follow you, have I? And are you then going to lower me down?"

Until that moment I had not realised that for a few minutes, for the first time, I had been leading the way. I had been so intent on what I was doing that the thought had not occurred to me. I had a moment of purely selfish delight. To be first on the rope! It was something that certainly would not happen to me very often, and I had not even noticed! . . . Later, when that outing was over, Piraly said to me: "When I watched you starting up I wondered very much how you'd get on. Because, you know, a girl with eyesight wouldn't have dared climb like that, she'd have been too frightened. I'm very pleased with you, and I'm still rather amazed at the skill and ease with which you did it."

These words from my guide and friend filled me with happiness. I had climbed that little wall of ice because I wanted to. I had thought and calculated and felt that I could do it. I knew that if I had not made the attempt I should always have regretted it.

Life is often like that. When one has the feeling that a door is open, that there is a something which one can do, then one has to try it, although it may be something one has never done before. At such moments confidence and hopefulness are all that matter. Stars bright as suns often shine for us in the sky and we don't know it—we are afraid to believe in them . . .

Piraly and I ended that excursion with other exercises as enjoyable as they were practical; and before returning to the Nid d'Aigle we shared an orange which I put in the snow to cool after peeling it. It was delicious.

That evening we went down to Houches by the Belle Vue cable-line and called on Maurice, our last year's team-mate. He was the same as ever, busy with his films and cameras, dreaming of the heights, but with no sense of time when it came to estimating how long it would take to reach any given place . . .

Those hours at Bionnassay were among the happiest in my life because they taught me something about climbing of which I had had too little experience, the meaning of real action, active participation in the life of the rope-team.

I must again express my immense gratitude to Monsieur Piraly and to all the climbing friends, near and far, who have so greatly helped me, despite all the trouble I have given them.

Returning from those calm and distant regions one has a sense of being cleansed and purified; it gives one the courage to go on living so that one may one day revisit those heights where the snow is to white and beautiful and pure . . .

PART TWO

UNDERGROUND

I

In the Wake of Elisabeth Casteret

I<small>T</small> seems to me impossible to add a new chapter to the literature
of speleology without first paying tribute to Elisabeth Casteret,
who died in 1940 giving birth to her fifth child. She was a model
among explorers as she was among mothers, one we must strive to
emulate, the tale of whose achievements in the great caverns of
France and Morocco can be read and re-read. Truly the Great Lady
of speleology, who held the first record established by a woman for
exploration underground. It gave me great pleasure, a few days
ago, to receive a letter from her husband, Monsieur Norbert
Casteret, in which he said: "This is to assure you of my warm
sympathy, since you are my spiritual daughter in speleology."

Why caves? The reader may well be astonished, after hearing so
much about my love of mountain heights. But the strange and
marvellous contrast is one that I cherish. My life is made up of
contrasts, and I personally find nothing surprising in this descent
from the heights to the depths. It seems to me to follow quite
naturally, to be a logical part of my destiny, although in this case
I had great good fortune.

Peaks and caverns are parts of the same mirror, which is the
earth. It is a mirror with two faces and I ardently longed to know
them both. Indeed I was fascinated by the subterranean world
before I came to love the mountains, because it seemed to me more
mysterious, more unknown and therefore more alluring. That I
came to know the mountains first is simply due to the fact that for
ten years my holidays took me to the Alps.

To me these two great passions of my life are like twin sisters,
each complementing the other. The writings of Norbert Casteret,
which I read with avidity in my ceaseless desire for knowledge,
taught me to love the mountains; and the knowledge of climbing

which I acquired was of great help to me in underground exploration.

On the advice of Monsieur Casteret, who has done a great deal of mountaineering, I shall not attempt to strike a balance between those two splendid fields of adventure, which constitute one whole, and to both of which I have given my whole heart.

As children in our Versailles garden my brother and I had dug tunnels in the sand. We did it with great seriousness, propping and staying our excavations before finally we demolished them, sole masters of the small caves we made. And we invented long, exciting tales of which, needless to say, we were the heroes.

"We're in a passage deep underground and we follow it a long, long way and in the end we come to a door, and it leads to an underground castle full of treasure . . ."

There was Marie-Antoinette's cave in the grounds of the Petit Trianon at Versailles, different only in scale from the ones my brother and I made. It was closed when I was very small, and so I was never able to go into it, but hearing about it stirred my imagination. There were children's stories on the radio, which later prompted me to read the tales of Jules Verne; and at about the time when I was doing so there was a radio-documentary on the prehistoric caves, with their remarkable drawings, of La Vézère and Lascaux. I was filled with the desire to be a great explorer and discover caves, and I said to myself, "One of these days I will!"

I learnt about volcanoes, mountains and cave-dwellers at the Ecole Braille de Saint-Mandé, where I went to school. By the age of ten I was passionately interested in geology, and I transcribed into braille everything I could find out about the geological periods. I lay in bed in the dormitory dreaming of those remote ages in the history of the earth.

But our nights at Saint-Mandé, during the years 1943 and 1944, were liable to be restless ones. Air-raid warnings sometimes got us out of bed, to be taken down to the basement, as often as three times in a night. I can see myself now, half-asleep, tripping over the hem of my over-long nightgown, with a bundle of clothes wrapped in my blue school overall under my arm. The grown-ups hurried us up when we didn't go fast enough. I was frightened by the talk of raids and bombs. All the lights were out.

My brother and I played with other children of our age in the cellars of the apartment-house at Versailles where my parents lived. They were far less splendid than the school basement. One had to be constantly ducking one's head and bending double, besides being careful not to burn one's fingers with bad candles. But this was play, and not something we were made to do, and we had wonderful games of hide-and-seek.

I enjoyed those games because I was on equal terms with my playmates. I had no sense of inferiority when I was with them. They never made me feel inferior, although they were all children of about ten.

Like all of them, and perhaps better than the others, I knew the cellars and every nook and cranny of the five staircases in the building. I could always find the enemy. Those were very friendly and happy games.

When I was about twelve I was awarded as a prize a little book in braille entitled "Away with Fear!", by Norbert Casteret, the speleologist. I have it still. It is a very small part of Monsieur Casteret's works, but to me it is immensely precious and I return to it after fifteen years with as much pleasure as when I first read it. It is beside me as I write, and I must quote one sentence which has often helped me in my struggle to come to terms with blindness: "Courage, sometimes, is to feel afraid and be the only one to know it."

Norbert Casteret tells the story, in this little book, of a lively night in the Pradières cavern when he thought he was being pursued by evildoers who turned out, as he discovered the next day, to be nothing but a few sheep. It is a small masterpiece of observation and prehistoric evocation.

After reading it I set about reading the rest of Monsieur Casteret's works. I often re-read them, and I think I know nearly all of them. It was these writings which, from the time I was thirteen, caused my heart to tremble with the longing for adventure. That became my great secret, which I guarded even more jealously and privately than my love of mountains. I said to myself in those days, "Mountaineering is impossible for you." But did that apply to caves?

I knew that it would be difficult; I never delude myself. But I was firmly resolved that some day I would try the caves. I knew that I should have to wait a long time, but I waited, dreaming of them more and more.

When later I became a boarder at the Institution Nationale I often had a book on caves in my locker in the classroom or the music-room, stuffed in with books on geography or Mozart parts.

The blind have one great advantage over people who can see; they do not need a light to read by, since they do it with their fingers. Although it was against the rules I would hide a book under my bed-clothes in dormitory and read far into the night.

Let me hasten to say, for the benefit of the teachers who always awarded me top marks for good conduct, that these transgressions, which I now confess to, were wholly occasioned by my interest in mountaineering and cave-exploration. If anyone is to be punished, it should be the authors of those enthralling books! And I may add that my reading in no way harmed my school work. On the contrary, it added enormously to the interest of the laboratory where we were taught about stalactites and the other mineral formations caused by the seeping of water into caves. Our teacher also showed us flints shaped by stone-age men, and from the day he did so, in the autumn of 1951, I longed to possess one.

Heaven knows how often I explored caves in imagination before I did so in reality. I followed the heroes of the books I read along great galleries and narrow tunnels, into chasms and through halls vast as cathedrals. I was one with them, and I infinitely admired Madame Elisabeth Casteret.

With Norbert Casteret I discovered underground streams and heard their different voices, from that of the humble stream in the Montsaunes cave to that of the subterranean River Lunain at Villemer. I had not visited any of them, or the caves either, but I cannot tell you how much I loved them.

I was not afraid of that underground world. To read about it was an escape, a wonderful release; and I found as I turned the pages that I had much in common with the people who had explored it.

One evening at Versailles, about eight years ago, I sat reading the text of a book of magnificent photographs taken by Norbert Casteret, with the title, "What I have seen Underground". This time I had an overwhelming feeling (I nearly wrote "revelation") that one day I would become a cave-explorer. I read the following:

"The extraordinary beauty of that underground world, and of the natural phenomena evolving in eternal darkness, is a hundred-fold rewarding. It may illumine a whole lifetime with the memory of unimaginable hours passed in a solitude unknown on the surface of the earth."

Months went by, and in 1957 I had the honour and great happiness of becoming numbered among Monsieur Casteret's correspondents. It came about very simply. I wrote and asked for a complete list of his works. He gave me much more—both advice, which I have found invaluable, and a fatherly friendship.

I could no longer doubt my vocation as a speleologist. But, as Monsieur Casteret has written, "Speleology calls for great patience", and "Patience is not weakness but the strength that endures".

At length the great day came. Monsieur Casteret invited me to visit him on his big estate facing the Pyrenees. My gratitude and delight can be imagined!

2

Labastide - the Cave of the Roaring Lion

O N 24th August, 1962 I left Saint-Gervais and the Alps for the Pyrenees. Although I had a comfortable couchette on the Pyrenees Express I found it impossible to sleep. The heat was stifling. At Grenoble they put on a steam locomotive which filled the compartment with smoke. We went through Valence and Avignon, and here I caught the good scent of eucalyptus. Nîmes–Montpellier–Sète . . . I dozed but did not really sleep. Although I love travelling I felt that the night would never end, and the train was horribly noisy.

We reached Narbonne two hours late and then had to wait a long time outside the station. The people on the platform cheered when at last we started again, and the station-master did not seem to enjoy the tribute. That journey was interminable!

I knew that Providence had been twenty-seven years preparing me for this great day, and that I must be patient. Toulouse–Muret– it seemed that I would never get there . . . And then at last it was Saint-Gaudens!

Monsieur Casteret was on the platform to meet me, and he greeted me as my father might have done on my homecoming. Everything was simple and natural, and I had no sense of being out of place. I felt as though we had always known each other, and we started talking about caves at once.

"Colette, I hope you're not too tired after your journey."

"No, not at all."

"Because I thought we might visit a cave this afternoon."

"I should love to. Which one?"

"I thought of Labastide. It seems exactly right for your first experience of caves."

Labastide! . . . It was the prehistoric cave of which Monsieur Casteret had written:

94

"Such discoveries, such rare joys reserved for the explorer, cause him quickly to forget the fatigues, the snares and the dangers of underground exploration."

We lunched at Castel Mourlon, on the bank of the River Dauphine, which flows towards the High Pyrenees, and then drove some twenty miles along the Bayonne road to Lannemesan. Here we turned south towards the village of Labastide, driving along the Neste through bracken-covered downs. I had put on canvas overalls, thick socks and my mountaineering boots—a real potholer's kit!

The time of dreaming was over. Monsieur Casteret, at the wheel of the car, talked to me in his quiet voice, describing the country-side he knew and loved so well. He was modesty itself; yet he is one of the great scholars of our time, a great researcher and a hero. And now, on this 25th August, 1962, I was to enter the remarkable cave he had discovered and explored in 1930 with Madame Casteret. It was extraordinary. That word has very little meaning, but I shall use it often in this account of my first underground expedition.

The little village of Labastide de Neste is situated in a deep valley. It was like another world, peaceful and happy, and one had a feeling that our noisy civilisation would never reach it, and so much the better. We parked the car in a farmyard after greeting the very friendly farmer and his wife. They were amazed at the thought that a blind girl could be passionately interested in caves. "Good Heavens!" they exclaimed.

We continued on foot. The cave was about a quarter of a mile from the village, and we had soon left the last house behind. I had taken Monsieur Casteret's arm. It was an easy walk, down into the silent depths of the valley.

The sun was very hot, but it would be cold when we got under-ground. The path was bordered with scented shrubs and walnut trees in whose branches birds were twittering. These unfamiliar surroundings strengthened me and prepared me, gently and maternally, as only Nature can do, for my entry into the great sanctuary.

Gradually my ears and mind became closed to the frantic, agitated tumult of the twentieth century. I felt that here I could live again, I so badly needed to be reborn to a new life.

We reached the end of the valley where, as though in a cradle, the stream has mysteriously wound its way and sung its song for thousands of years. It brought us to the Lower Chamber of Labastide, not very deep and lighted by the sun, where only the stream pursued its way into regions inaccessible to man.

"But can't we follow it?" I asked. "Perhaps it runs through wonderful, fairylike grottos."

"It flows underground for about two miles," said Monsieur Casteret, "and comes up at the village of Esparros, on the other side of the mountains. I've only been able to follow it a third of the way. The rest is unexplored."

In fact, he had been there for the first time thirty-two years ago, and had waded through the cold water I was now touching with my hand along the low rock-tunnel stretching ahead of us. Then he had followed a wide corridor giving access to a chamber where at the time there was a dangerous concentration of carbon dioxide. He had come back a month later and had succeeded in getting as far as a deep underground lake of which the outlet was a narrow and impassable siphon, or sump.

"If you like we'll go to the Upper Cave. We have to climb a hundred-foot slope and then go down about sixty feet of loose rock to reach the grille."

"You mean there's an iron grille?"

"Yes. We decided we'd have to put one in, although it was a very difficult job, to protect the cave against vandalism and the damage certain people were doing it. It contains masterpieces of prehistoric art. A number of caves are protected in this way, although in this case the protection is not very effective, as you'll see."

At the bottom of the debris we found ourselves under a majestic vault which may have been fifty feet wide. It was cold, and this came as a shock, after the stifling heat outside. A permanent mist pervaded the great porch, caused by the intermingling of two currents of air.

We paused here to rest. It was time to light the acetylene lamp. Monsieur Casteret knelt down to do so, and I knelt as well.

Everything in me was appeased. Souls entering Paradise after having so long aspired to it must know, multiplied to infinity, that same sense of quietude.

Norbert Casteret greeting Colette Richard after her solitary bivouac underground

In a hole

A leg up

I now heard drops of water falling from the rocky ceiling—my first drops! That music was just what I had always imagined it to be.

We went on to the grille, which was very handsome with a relief inscription, so that I could read the letters with my finger—"Labastide, M H F" (Monument Historique Français).

But as a barrier the grille was less efficient than it was impressive to look at. There were gaps which greatly distressed Monsieur Casteret; three places where it did not completely fill the splendid romanesque archway of the entrance.

"So you're going to visit your first cave by breaking the law!" he said, laughing, as I performed a small feat of acrobatics to wriggle between the iron bars and the wall.

We were in a huge gallery which we followed for over fifty yards to by-pass a wide fissure.

"Give me your hand. On your right there's a horse carved in the rock. The muzzle is deeply incised and the outline is very delicate. I want you to feel it."

Monsieur Casteret took my hand and I made contact with my first prehistoric work of art. An artist of the Magdalenian period had created it twenty thousand years before. Twenty thousand years . . . twenty times ten centuries . . . and it was still intact! I could feel the exact shape of the horse's muzzle beneath my finger-tips. I stayed there a long time touching it and conjuring up the picture in my mind. I was deeply moved.

We were now in absolute darkness, wholly dependent on our small lamp with its vivid flame, by the light of which we would have to find our way back. Supposing it went out? The thought did not trouble me for a moment. I was holding Monsieur Casteret's rucksack and could thus follow him to the end of the world. It was the method I had used in the mountains: a hand resting on the rucksack of my guide, or holding his belt, which enabled me to know instinctively what movement to make next.

We made our way along a rough and slippery earth-slope which ended in a wide horizontal corridor, where however we still had to climb over piles of fallen debris and go round boulders.

I found that I was speaking in a hushed voice, although I tried not to. Whenever Monsieur Casteret said anything to me I answered in a half-whisper. This place was like a sanctuary or a church.

Coming out of the twentieth century I felt ashamed of breaking a silence so filled with precious memories.

Presently we came to an obstruction, a huge mass of rock fallen from the roof thousands of years before, on which prehistoric men had drawn a horse six feet long in red paint, its stiff mane tinted black. Unfortunately I could not touch it because it was too high.

"But how were they able to paint things so high up in those days?"

"Well, the Magdalenians built scaffolding. And a thing to note is that the only light they had came from lamps burning animal-fat or torches of juniper, which must have given off a lot of acrid smoke. They needed to keep a large stock of torches in the caves to supply themselves with that very feeble light!"

We passed round the left-hand side of the great boulder, where there was a small passageway leading to a shaft a hundred feet deep giving access to the stream in the lower cave. The corridor narrowed, growing steeper, until it became no more than a sort of gutter, a rough, narrow staircase up which I scrambled on all fours, which was great fun. Then it widened again, and as we went on Monsieur Casteret drew my attention to stalagmites and other limestone formations, some like draperies, which made me think of the robes of antique virgins. Some of these draperies had tilted slightly out of their original vertical position, which proved that the earth had shifted despite its apparent fixity.

We came to a little basin out of which I picked two pebbles as a souvenir. The cave was leading us ever deeper into the heart of the earth, inviting us to learn all its secrets. It was becoming very damp and decorated with beautiful formations.

"In another minute you'll be up to your knees in mud. This place is an absolute quagmire of clay and it's very slippery. I'm going to carry you."

I laughed a great deal as my companion slithered about the place, trying not to collapse under my weight. Pot-holers are all big children. One can't be fussy underground, where everyone has to help everyone else.

"Here's a little stalactite, Colette. Feel how elegant it is."

"It's rather rough but very pretty. And besides," I said, "it's my first stalactite."

"It's calcite. One finds an enormous variety of mineral concretions in caves. These in Labastide are not the most strange or the most beautiful . . . Feel this." Monsieur Casteret took my hand. "It's a little cylindrical hole bored naturally in the rock. We christened it the 'ball-race'. Our children used to play with it for hours when they were young, which left my wife and me free to explore the cave and make notes of what we found."

We moved on to our right, entering a chamber with a low ceiling. Here, Monsieur Casteret told me, the Magdalenians had surpassed themselves. The drawings were striking in their freshness and vigour. More than twenty thousand years ago . . . The words ran through my mind like a refrain . . .

"I want you to touch the mouth of the Roaring Lion . . . There . . . Follow the outline of the canine tooth with your finger. It's very well carved, very impressive—the man who carved it must certainly have seen that lion! To judge by the way he drew it he must have been horribly frightened!"

What Monsieur Casteret did not mention, in his modesty, was that he himself was the discoverer of that life-sized lion's head, in the place where it had been roaring for twenty thousand years. He had every right to be proud of it. I brushed my fingers lightly over the rock, not daring to press hard for fear of damaging a masterpiece. It was extraordinary to think that in the far, far distant past the fingers of my prehistoric brother, and his chisel of flint, had passed over that same surface. I was filled with awe.

The silence bore down on us, weighted with its age-old memories. One felt very small in the presence of so much grandeur and accumulated beauty. This was the meeting-place of God and Man and the centuries. I felt tears come into my eyes, and I imagined Monsieur Carteret's little lamp. Its soft, living light was the symbol of fire, the flame handed down to us which is also the Divine Presence in all places.

There were twelve more horses incised on the walls and the roof, of all sizes and intertwined according to a certain ritual. There were also two bison and two heads of sorcerers. Monsieur Casteret believed that the place must have served as a temple, for the ground seemed to have been trodden smooth by ritualistic dancing, and one of the sorcerers' heads completed the slender outline of a dancer in a posture recalling certain contemporary Negro dances.

We climbed a steep escarpment, and Monsieur Casteret roped me for fear I should slip. The place was curiously pitted with small holes formed by "piercing" drops of water. The clay was thus hollowed in little cylindrical cavities, each with a hard bottom which was the beginning of a stalagmite. Monsieur Casteret told me about all these things in a quiet, knowledgeable way which filled me with delight. This was one of the greatest days in my life, and I was deeply aware of it.

"We're now at the narrowest part of the cave," said Monsieur Casteret. "Further on there's a picture of a bird, a bustard. Birds figure very seldom in prehistoric drawings, and this one is certainly a bustard, not a goose. It's a bird that lived in cold climates at the time of the last Ice Age, when snowfields covered the country."

We followed an earth embankment flanking a shaft made by a stream that poured in through a hole above. The bed of the stream was dry at the time; there was very rarely water in it.

"A young engineer once got trapped in that shaft. He told me about it afterwards. He couldn't climb out, and his fiancée had to get out of the cave by herself and go to the village for help. He left his gloves and cigarettes at the bottom, and I found them there later . . . And here, on our left," Monsieur Casteret went on, "I found a prehistoric hearth with a horse's skull in the middle. There are stones round it which evidently served as seats. One wonders what kind of magical ceremonies those people enacted, but that is something we shall never know."

The roof came lower. Then we reached the last cave of the series, a huge chamber, sloping upwards and very earthy, where we sat down to rest. We ate biscuits and chocolate and talked about such things as claustrophobia and the mirages pot-holers sometimes see.

"I'll put out my lamp," said Monsieur Casteret, "and perhaps you'll be better able to 'feel the solitude' as an English major once said to me in this place."

Then there was absolute silence, broken only by the sound of falling drops of water which was already becoming dear to my newly-attuned ears. But there were not many of these because it was a dry year.

The silence did not worry me; indeed, I found it comforting. Before we entered the cave Monsieur Casteret had said: "People who aren't used to it sometimes find it disturbing, even crushing.

It's a kind of silence you can't find anywhere else. Everyone reacts differently to it."

In my case the warning was unnecessary. When he had lit the lamp again I said: "It's wonderful. I love silence. And I don't find this one crushing. It certainly isn't a silence of 'nothingness', as people are so fond of saying."

We rested for half an hour and then started back the way we had come. When we reached the rock with the red horse we climbed up so that I could touch some of the other carvings. There were two horses, a reindeer and a young rhinoceros without a horn, its eye more deeply incised than the rest of its body—all in an admirable state of preservation. I tried to fix them all in my mind so that I would never forget them.

After this we returned to the entrance—and Heavens, how quickly the time had passed!

We took off our steel helmets, glorious relics of the 1914 war and glorious also for the underground expeditions in which they had taken part. Then we sat down at the edge of the stream and carefully cleaned our boots with the help of sprigs of mint that scented our hands. There was an especial pleasure, unknown to other people, in thus returning to the light of day, our overalls stained with mud and impregnated with the scent of clay which later was to fill me with nostalgia.

While we drove to Mourlon I made notes in braille of my first impressions of the exciting world I had just entered. It was hard to believe that we had spent three hours underground. I had thought it no more than one. I felt renewed, physically and morally re-generated. My previous existence seemed very far away. I had been born to a new life.

The sun was setting, and as it lay red on the horizon I became a child of the mountains of Comminges.

We returned later to Labastide with Jacques Jolfre, a charming companion and an expert photographer. We also took my small transistorised tape-recorder to preserve a sound-record of our doings.

Our first operation was my descent by an "electron" steel-wire ladder into the Labastide chasm, a wide pit fifty or sixty feet deep. Monsieur Casteret was anxious for me to do this as an exercise before I tackled bigger descents.

Jacques fixed the ladder to a large boulder, using steel tackle specially designed for the purpose. Then he unrolled it and let it down into the trough while I was being roped and Monsieur Casteret was giving me my instructions.

"I've got you well secured. Move slowly backwards to the edge. That's it. Now kneel down with your legs on either side of the ladder and your hands on the rungs."

"Am I in the right position?"

"Yes, you're fine. Keep on going backwards. On your stomach now. Press yourself against the ladder and make sure of your grip as you go over the edge."

I made a great stillness within me. I had dreamed all my life of making a descent like this. The ladder was extremely slender, the steel rungs about seven inches wide, so that there was only room for one foot on a rung. It was alarming but very exciting.

Jacques was getting his camera ready and keeping an eye on my movements, which Monsieur Casteret could not see because of the overhang.

"Say something," he said. "All the tape-recorder is registering is silence."

"Well, my hands are full of clay."

"That doesn't matter. Go on."

"I can't find rungs for my feet."

"Feel round for them. They're there."

"I can't find them. My feet are just dangling."

"They're all the same distance apart."

"Ah, now I've got one."

"Good, Keep going, and take it easy."

"Oh, it's revolving!"

"What is?"

"The ladder!"

"Never mind. Carry on."

"It's queer. I'm well away from the wall and I'm spinning round."

"Are you giddy?"

"Yes."

"Frightened?"

"Yes."

"Stop!" interrupted Jacques. "I want to take a photo. Turn towards me."

"I can't. Whenever I try to move the ladder in any direction it starts revolving, but always the opposite way."

At length, after a good deal of spinning, I was able to keep the ladder still for a few moments and Jacques got two snapshots, as I knew by the flashes.

"Do you want to go on or are you getting tired?"

"I'm all right."

Steadying myself as best I could on that spidery ladder I went down a few more rungs. But then, when I was about halfway, there was a hitch.

"Something's gone wrong," I said. "I can't move."

"What's the trouble?"

"My left foot seems to have got stuck. I can't shake it free."

"Well, don't shake too hard. Climb up again if you can't go on down."

"I can't do that either. And my left foot's lower than my right, so I can't reach down and disengage it. I think the studs on my climbing-boot must have got caught in the ladder."

"We should have thought of that. Those studs are often a nuisance."

"Well, what am I to do?"

"Just be patient and try to work your foot loose. And don't be afraid. The rope will hold you whatever happens."

I made fruitless efforts to release my foot while the ladder revolved more than ever. I began to feel tired and exasperated, and the rope under my arms was cutting into me. After a time I gave up, and wrapping my arms round the ladder hung like that for a moment, resting. I could hear talk going on above my head. The two men were wondering whether to climb down to me or whether it would be better to haul me up. They decided on the latter course.

"We'll bring you up by hauling both the ladder and the rope."

"I don't like the sound of that."

"There's no other way."

It was all rather alarming and very slow, and I decided that I would not make any more ladder descents. The rope tightened under my armpits. I gave a sudden jerk and exclaimed: "My foot's come free!"

"Fine. Well, do you want to come back or go on down?"

"I'm not sure."

"Then go on down," said Monsieur Casteret. "You'll be glad afterwards."

"All right."

I went on gingerly, getting my feet caught several times, until I found that the best method was to rest only the toe of my boot on the rung and move fast. At length I cried: "I'm there!"

"Good. Now you can have a rest."

I sat on a rock and waited. Fragments of gravel falling on my head—or to be exact, on my helmet—told me that someone was on their way to join me. It was Monsieur Casteret. We then climbed up again together.

"Not a very happy first attempt," he said. "You must try again, to give yourself confidence. But this time roll your stockings down over your boots so that the studs won't get hitched up in the ladder."

I obediently did as I was told, without enthusiasm and indeed with some apprehension. But this time all was well. I got down without any trouble and was very pleased with myself. Jacques took several photographs, and I hoped that one day I would descend into a real abyss.

We were now all in high spirits, and we explored the big cavern in search of new manoeuvres for me to practise and photographs for Jacques to take.

"Here's something. Put your hand here."

"What is it? It's icy! It feels very queer under my fingers."

"It's a bat in its winter sleep. They sleep upside down hanging by their feet. If you lift it up gently you can hold it in your hand."

"Why, it's ringed!"

"Yes—Number ZL 8682."

"My first bat! It's not at all frightening. It has very soft fur and it feels very fragile."

I held the little creature gently in my hand, warming it, stroking it, spreading out one of its wings and brushing it against my cheek to feel the softness of its furry covering. To disprove the old wives' tale I even put it on my head. It made no attempt to pull out my hair with its slender claws. I studied it for a long time while Monsieur Casteret talked about its skill in flight and the sense of direction which amounted to a sixth sense. This was something hard to understand, and I was envious. The bat did not need a white stick to warn it of obstacles in its path!

"There's a good surface!" said Jacques. "I'd like a photograph of you up there."

"But how am I to get up?"

"Nothing easier," said Monsieur Casteret. "You can climb up on my shoulders."

So I got on his shoulders with my big, muddy boots. I felt that I must be very heavy and I was afraid of hurting him; but I was even more afraid of slipping and falling. There was no secure handhold; everything was sticky with clay. While I was struggling Jacques fixed a new magnesium flash and gave me highly picturesque advice.

"I haven't finished yet," he said when he had made the first exposure. "Go on climbing."

"Only if Monsieur Casteret will help me. It's practically vertical."

"Not really. It just feels like that."

"Don't cling on with your knees," said Monsieur Casteret. "Lean back. More still. Just relax. It's a childishly easy climb. Lift your left foot six inches. That's it. On your right there's a stalagmite that will hold your other foot."

"But suppose it doesn't hold!"

"Don't worry, it's been holding since the beginning of the world. It'll last a few more millennia."

"Provided the end of the world doesn't come this afternoon!"

The silly things one says when one is underground!

"Heavens! I'm slipping—I've fallen!"

"You should have said, 'I want to fall'!"

The climb ended in general laughter. We went on along the cave until we noticed a hole on our right.

"Where does that lead to?"

"It's just a cat-hole that doesn't lead anywhere. I've never been along it."

"Then how do you know it doesn't lead anywhere?"

"I don't think it does. You can try if you like. You'll be the first person to explore it."

I instantly accepted the challenge. It might be a hole of no importance, but at least it was one that no one had ventured into before me. I wriggled on my stomach for some yards. It was very narrow. Naturally I had not got a lamp, and I could not even detect the glow of my companions' lamps as they stood in the lofty gallery behind me.

"Well? Can you go on? Have you discovered anything?"

"I can still go on. It's blocked directly ahead, with clay and a few stalagmites. But it goes on to the left. There's a faint draught. It turns into a sort of wide passage, but the ceiling's still very low. I've still got to wriggle. I'm wondering . . ."

"What about?"

"I have an idea that it must lead into another big cave."

"Well, it may lead into the Cave of the Horses and the Roaring Lion."

"Do you think so? But suppose it's an undiscovered cave?"

"No, from the general topography I'd say it's bound to be the Roaring Lion."

Monsieur Casteret followed me, and we presently found that he was right. I was rather disappointed.

"Still, you've achieved something," Monsieur Casteret said. "You've found a communicating passage that I didn't know about."

It was a sop to my beginner's pride.

Finally the three of us sat down to rest in the depths of the beautiful Labastide cave. Monsieur Casteret held us enthralled with tales of his early subterranean expeditions. He ended by rising to his feet and reciting, in the "great black silence", the cave-explorer's prayer written by his friend, the poet Ralph Parrot.

3

The Riousec Cave, Haute-Garonne

WE got up early the day after my arrival to attend Mass at Saint-Gaudens before starting on our next expedition. It was a Sunday and very fine. We were joined by Jacques Jolfre, who has a particularly good knowledge of the Riousec cave.

Jacques Jolfre, an ardent explorer of the region who has done much to arouse the interest of young people in pot-holing, had been one of the team who, that spring, had reached the bottom of the Pierre Saint-Martin chasm, a depth of nearly 3000 feet. He is a tall, forthright young man, modest and extremely likeable. The darkness and silence prevailing underground make him disinclined to talk over-much about the things he has seen and discovered in the depths; and that is the attitude of the true explorer.

South of Saint-Gaudens we followed the Aspet road and then that of the Pyrenees, well known for its great passes. We drove through the foothills of the Pyrenees, amid woods and meadows. Fleecy clouds overhung the peaks and in the distance Mount Cagire was to be seen, a peak of about 6000 feet containing the cave of the same name. I was particularly interested in it because it was in this cave that Monsieur Casteret had found some wonderful pisolites or peastones, also known as "cave pearls", which are very rare. Then we came in sight of the Massif d'Arbas, culminating in Mont Paloumère, a peak of something over 5000 feet.

"That range is famous," said Monsieur Casteret, "particularly since we explored the Henne-Morte and Coume-Ouarnède caves."

We were very talkative, delighted to be setting out on an adventure, from which one always returns stronger and happier. I thought of the remedial qualities of certain caves; of the Klutert cave, for example, which is good for asthma, and the radio-active cave at Bad Gastein in Germany, which is said to cure rheumatism and other ailments. However this may be, I am convinced, and always will be, that caves are places for the easing of body and soul, provided one is not afraid of that underground world.

I questioned my companions closely about what it was like at the bottom of the Pierre Saint-Martin chasm. Were there no big caves leading out of it, no extensions of any kind? I so wanted it to be the deepest abyss in the world! . . . We also talked about the Gouffre Raymonde, with its thermal springs, and about E. A. Martel, the first great speleologist, who was employed on a research mission by the Ministry of Agriculture and explored this region in 1908 and 1909.

We went uphill, following the rapids of a little river called the Ger, and pulled up at an altitude of 2500 feet to go and inspect "La Buhadère", a hole about the size of a man's body. An icy wind blows out of it. "Blows" is the right word, because the name "Buhadère" signifies the act of blowing. The stream of air is so strong that it will keep a handkerchief streaming horizontally.

"It must lead to a big cave," I said. "Has it been explored?"

"Some young men cleared the opening. It has been partly explored."

"What's it like inside?"

"First there's a sloping passage that one has to crawl along and then some very deep basins. It probably communicates with the Riousec cave and the resurgence of a stream."

I was kneeling in front of the windy hole, and I would have stopped there a long time if my companions had not gently reminded me that I was in danger of catching cold. I had done the same thing a few years before at a "blowing hole" in the Massif Central scarcely large enough for a cat to get through. I was already cave-minded and dreaming of prehistory . . .

We finally left the car at the Col du Portet d'Aspet and followed a path which wound up the mountainside amid bracken, box, conifers and hart's tongue. Monsieur Casteret, who was leading the way, handed me leaves and flowers to identify. Every minute spent in his company was instructive, as Jacques would be the first to agree.

My companions picked small, delicately-scented roses for me, and wild carnations such as I had found in the Alps and in the disused quarry where I had played as a child. Jacques talked about the inflatable boat he was making for future subterranean exploration.

"I'm going to try it out on the River Aliou," he said. "The Medusa passage isn't too difficult, is it?"

Monsieur Casteret answered our questions with inexhaustible patience. We were insatiable!

"What are the mountains you can see on the horizon?"

"I can see the frontier-ridge with the Pic Crabère, over 8000 feet high, which is the geographical centre of the Pyrenees and marks the division between the departments of Ariège and Haute Garonne. It's equidistant from the Atlantic and the Mediterranean. Then there's the Maubermé with the Martel chasm and the splendid Cigalère grotto. Then Mont Vallier and all the peaks of the Ariège. And on our right there's the Massif d'Arbas, a range where very few people go and which is not well known. One has to cut one's way through dense undergrowth."

"There must be a lot of unexplored parts of that range."

"There certainly are. We realise it every time we discover a new pot-hole. It's the land of caves."

We walked for nearly an hour, talking all the time, in the shade of a slendid forest of beech trees. Then Jacques, who had taken the lead, turned off the path and climbed a very steep slope covered with dead leaves and moss. He threw me a rope and I climbed up after him without any trouble. Monsieur Casteret followed.

We were outside the Riousec cave, at a height of about 4000 feet, which is seldom visited and hard to find. A current of very cold air came out of the entrance, which was not unlike that of Labastide. Since it was nearly midday we settled down away from the draught to have lunch before going inside.

Riousec was inhabited in Neolithic times. Jacques had found fragments of pottery and a polished stone axe-head within a hundred yards of the entrance. And Monsieur F. Trombe, who made a map of the cave, had the good fortune to find a large piece of Neolithic pottery completely intact.

Before entering we hung up our rucksacks, after taking what we needed out of them, and lighted our acetylene lamps. The deeper we penetrated into the cave, the stronger and colder did the wind become. There was no iron grille here, as in Labastide. We walked for the first hundred and fifty yards along a wide, level "entrance-hall", passing on our right a passageway leading to a shaft some thirty feet deep, which we were to return to later.

Jacques went first. We negotiated a long, rock-encumbered downward slope to reach the "lobby", the crossroads of this vast, chaotic cave-system which is in no way comparable to Labastide. From here we first visited the Great Hall, which Monsieur Trombe has christened "Chamber A".

Once again I was enthralled by the wonderful atmosphere of the caves, although this was only the second I had visited. The clay smelt so good. I was grateful to Monsieur Casteret for bringing me to solitary caverns which sightseers and rowdy parties had not yet robbed of their silence. I held on to his belt, to which his lamp was fixed, and we picked our way through the chaos of that vaulted chamber of which the walls were lost in darkness.

"One could easily get lost in here," he remarked. "There's nothing to steer by. One has to find one's way as one goes. But that doesn't seem to be worrying you?"

"Not so long as you're here."

"If our lamps were to fail I can assure you we should never get out. I'm going to set fire to a newspaper. It'll give us a bit more light for a few moments and I'll have a chance to get my bearings."

On our right the slope vanished into nothingness. It was composed of more or less solid debris.

The drops of water which we liked so much were falling in abundance. We kept on moving upwards through the vast cavern which reminded me of the moraines on alpine glaciers, through which I had so often ploughed my way holding my guide's rucksack. I had never liked those moraines because the uncertain foothold worried me. Heaven knows how many miles of rubbly surface I had crossed on my way to the great peaks. And now I had my reward. I liked that "underground moraine" of Riousec, as I called it. I felt at home and in my element, and was far less disturbed by it than one might suppose. Later Monsieur Casteret was to say to some friends: "I was quite cross at Riousec when Colette said, 'It's easier than mountaineering!' I thought I'd found her a difficult cave!"

We went steadily on. As in the mountains I took care not to slip, not to loosen stones and not to let my team-mates get several paces ahead of me, thus avoiding falls on the craggy boulders.

That silent subterranean climb was utterly absorbing. Veering constantly to the left we were moving upward towards the roof. We had to perform all kinds of gymnastic feats, to climb boulders, sit down and slide, to jump fissures. The cavern was like a huge and very cold cathedral, with drops of water constantly falling—the ticking clock of eternity.

How could those tiny drops have produced this immense emptiness and chaos? Great cataclysms must have occurred here in the course of the ages. The more I thought of that immemorial past the more was I filled with awe and respect for our beautiful Earth which could so easily crush me.

"There are the most wonderful stalactites," said my companion. "Feel how smooth they are!"

There were formations of every shape and size, and I reflected that I was perhaps the first person ever to have touched them. It is a delight that all explorers know, and now in a small way I was one of them.

At length we reached the side and roof of the cave. I knew we were approaching them before the two men could see them with their lamps. The blind are accustomed to sense obstacles at a distance, and this faculty is enhanced underground. We had climbed more than a hundred yards of the most chaotic boulders imaginable, and were now close to a stalagmite of huge proportions. I learnt every detail of it with my finger while Jacques went on a little way to explore a stream at a lower level.

Monsieur Casteret and I sat down to rest. Not that we were really tired, but underground one has to conserve one's strength. We talked a little, but for the most part preferred to listen to the silence. The falling drops of water gave out different muscial notes. Our favourite topics of conversation were the geological periods, the infinity of Time and Space, God, Creation and Eternity . . . Such subjects were appropriate to the setting; but in the presence of so much grandeur and majesty we often preferred to keep silent and put out the light in order to meditate . . .

Presently Jacques returned to us.

"I want to go some distance along the stream," he said, in his charming local accent, "and see what happens to it further on. The water's very low. I shall be back in about two and a half hours."

"Have you enough fuel for your lamp?" asked Monsieur Casteret, being very experienced in the problems of solitary exploration. "Don't do anything rash. I know I need not say that to you, but all the same, when one is alone in a stream for a long spell one has to be careful."

"Don't worry."

"Well, good luck. We'd better agree to meet at the entrance, so as to be sure of finding each other."

Monsieur Casteret and I decided to visit the other part of the cave, and so, after Jacques had set off along the stream we started to pick our way through the rocky wilderness. I had taken off my watch, as I did in the mountains, so as to forget the passing of time and really escape from the everyday world.

Every now and then Monsieur Casteret had to stop. It was not because he had lost his way, he said, but because in that huge jumble of boulders which all looked very much alike he had to take his bearings every few yards, calculate levels and try to foresee possible obstacles. All this went on automatically in his mind, while at the same time he counted his steps to estimate distances. He was so accustomed to the darkness that it did not at all dismay him when he found that he had gone too far, so that we had to turn back and search again for what is conventionally called the right road. I asked no questions in order not to disturb his navigation.

My mind was busy and I was taking note of everything. I was glad to find that my pace underground exactly matched Monsieur Casteret's. The boulders were extremely resonant, and I could hear him clearly when he put down his foot and carefully tested a foothold to make sure that it was firm. He had that particular skill in his feet which I have already talked about in connection with mountaineering. He moved slowly and with care, and I hung on to his belt or his shoulder, and so we made our way through that pitch-black immensity.

Now and then he seated himself on a downward slope and slid, and I did likewise, just as I had done in the mountains, where Piraly and other team-mates had commented unkindly on the uncouthness of my methods. I thought of my mountaineering friends in those moments. They would certainly not have been happy underground, as they had told me. But I owed them a great deal and was deeply grateful to them. Monsieur Casteret also mentioned my climbing experience, saying that what I had learnt in the mountains would be of great value to me underground.

"Well, here we are, back in the anti-chamber," said Monsieur Casteret. "We've plenty of time to visit the other part of the system, the Salle Trombe, because I'm sure Jacques will be in no hurry to leave his stream."

"Do you think he'll try to get through the sump?"

"No, I'm sure he won't. One doesn't attempt a sump single-handed, particularly when it's a dangerous one and goes very deep."

"What a shame."

"In cave exploration one must always persevere bravely. You know our motto, *Ad augusta per angusta*—to great things by narrow paths."

The Trombe Cavern, which we had now entered, was no less chaotic than the other, but it was not so cold and the going seemed to me firmer.

"What is the reason for that?" I asked.

"It's because the slabs of rock here are covered with a stalagmitic deposit which binds them together."

"One feels very safe here," I said. "It's hard to believe that the whole thing could collapse in a few seconds."

"It has lasted a good many thousand years, as one can tell from the deposits. There's no reason why it should collapse this afternoon."

The walls and roof were again invisible, and they gave out a fine echo. We seemed to be climbing a mountain-peak. Indeed, that is what it was, on a small scale—a pile of loose rock several hundred feet high rising in the middle of that magnificent vaulted chamber, which was less complex in shape than the one we had left.

We sat down when we reached the summit, and I succumbed to an irristible impulse to throw stones in every direction and listen to the echo and try to make myself giddy by measuring the depth that surrounded us. Why is it that anyone on the edge of a precipice or chasm cannot resist throwing stones? It is a gesture as old as mankind. Monsieur Casteret was doing the same thing. We certainly had plenty of stones to play with.

The acetylene lamp showed signs of giving out, making strange sounds while the flame flickered and smoked. By careful nursing Monsieur Casteret persuaded it to give us just enough light to guide us back to the entrance.

While he was attending to it, still seated on our mountain of huge boulders, I amused myself by dropping different-sized pebbles into the gaps between them to get some idea of the dimensions of the hollows beneath our feet, which we had no other means of judging. It came as a shock to me to discover that the stones fell a very long way in that monstrous heap of rock debris.

On our way back to the "lobby" I thought of other caves described by Monsieur Casteret in his writings. His account of them had made a vivid impression on my mind, and I think I now recalled them because, after all, the terrifying nature of the caves we had just visited, the effect of extreme chaos, earth and rock in torment, had somewhat shaken me. There was one in particular, and I asked Monsieur Casteret if he could tell me which it was.

"Perhaps you're thinking of the Martel chasm, which my wife and I explored. It was very dangerous. During one of our expeditions there was a big fall of earth and we lost part of our equipment, but fortunately no member of the team was injured."

From the "lobby" we went on to visit a recess just below the thirty-foot shaft communicating with the "entrance hall". Here there were bones to be found—sheep's skulls, jawbones, skeletons of small creatures which had reached this place by accident and perished.

"Colette, I'm going to leave you here for a little while, and go and see what's happened to Jacques. Mind you don't wander too far away."

"I won't."

I made use of the minutes of solitude to get to know the place where he had left me. It was a blind-alley, its walls damp like everywhere else. The floor was almost level for some yards, but I was surrounded by enormous boulders.

I could still hear the sound of dripping water. I was happy to be in that place. Suddenly it occurred to me that I had an indelible pencil in my pocket, and for the first time in my life I wrote my initials on an untouched wall, in that small corner unknown to other dwellers on our planet, where the passing of a thousand years would not efface it . . .

Then I heard Monsieur Casteret coming back, and I thought I would play a little joke on him. I had noticed a rocky outcrop on my left that was more than big enough to hide me. I crouched behind it.

"I couldn't hear Jacques or see his light," said Monsieur Casteret, "but he's bound to be along soon . . . But where are you? Colette! Colette! What's happened?"

Hidden behind my rock I was laughing so much that I should have found it difficult to answer. I listened with delight while Monsieur Casteret went on calling me in his calm voice, in which I thought I detected a hint of anxiety.

"I'm certain," he said, "that there's no other way out. Well, really . . ."

He was getting close, and I knew that I should soon be spotted. I made myself as small as I could. He stopped as he drew near, and I exploded with laughter when he found me.

"So she went and hid herself—like a bat!" he said.

We made our way back to the entrance, following a low passage from which we threw stones down the shaft over my hiding-place. As we were doing so we heard Jacques calling in the distance, and we all met in the "entrance hall" with the wind blowing along it.

Outside it was blazingly hot. We were an hour's walk from the Col de Portet, and again we followed the Chemin des Gardes through that enchanted region of foothills. Jacques told us about his exploration of the stream.

"After leaving you I made for the end of the shaft where the stream comes out. It communicates with the upper Burtech chasm. The junction between the Burtech and the Riousec—a difference in level of about seven hundred feet—was effected by the Army in 1948. To reach the bed of the stream I had to climb down a forty-foot sheer face. The corridor's very narrow. I worked my way upstream for about seventy yards, but then the ceiling came down to a few inches above the water-level and I had to take off my clothes."

I pictured Jacques hanging his garments on a projecting rock and performing feats of acrobatics in that low, narrow tunnel enclosing the stream, wriggling along it on hands and knees.

"I managed to get through the conduit, which is about ten feet long. It must be full in times of flood."

"What was the temperature of the water?"

"Six or seven degrees."

"And what happened after that?"

"There's a passage about seventy yards long and two feet wide which leads into a bigger water-system."

"What's it like?" I asked impatiently.

"It's very much bigger. Upstream there's a steep rise, and downstream there's a pool about seven yards wide which seemed very deep. Beyond it the watercourse continues. That was all I could discover, because I hadn't the equipment for getting through the pool."

"But where does the stream go to?"

"We know that," said Monsieur Casteret. "We dyed the water with fluorescein and found that it joins the Oeil-Bleu two miles further on, at a depth of about 2000 feet. But most of its course is unknown and perhaps always will be, because it contains at least one impassable sump and there may be others."

"It would be wonderful if it could be explored. And if it were to turn out that Riousec communicates with La Buhadère, what a marvellous hydro-geological breakthrough that would be!"

"Unfortunately it is not given to us to know everything. Exploration is often slow and disappointing, which is why one must never give up."

At the Col de Portet we paid a call on the Martin family who run a hostel that is well known to pot-holers visiting the Massif d'Arbas. The place was full of light-hearted tourists, and a Basque who sang and danced added a touch of local colour.

We must have looked strange in our clay-stained overalls, but this did not prevent us from enjoying a most refreshing local drink made partly from almonds, the *orgeat* of the Spanish Pyrenees.

We had come from another world, but the people on Sunday outings could not have been happier than we, they who had never known the joy and exaltation of subterranean adventure . . .

Truly life is worth living, if only for the sake of such a day. I was thinking of this when Monsieur Casteret hung a sheep-bell round my neck as a souvenir. It has a very pleasant ring, and for the sake of contrast it will always have a place in the little glass-fronted cabinet where I keep thousand-year-old stalactites and chiselled flints.

4

The Underground River of Labouiche

On 27th August we left Saint-Gaudens at eight o'clock with a big programme ahead of us—two caves in Ariège. We drove along the Toulouse road, passing the village of Saint Martory, where Monsieur Casteret was born, and the Escalère caves, overlooking the Garonne, and Montsaunes with its ancient church, once a head-quarters of the Templars. There was a cave at Montsaunes which I had often dreamed of visiting, but it was now blocked.

We entered the Salat valley, which leads to Ariège, and passed through Saint-Girons, where the Lez flows into the Salat.

"The Lez," said Monsieur Casteret, "is the stream that flows out of the Cigalère cave."

"The subterranean river with fifty-two falls! It must be very noisy . . . Where have we got to now?"

"We're just coming to the fork in the road which leads to the Trois-Frères and Tuc d'Audoubert caves, about three miles from here, which were mapped by Count Begouen and his sons."

"Can't we go there?"

"We've got plenty to do as it is. One can't do everything."

"When were those caves discovered?"

"The Tuc-d'Audoubert was discovered in 1912. A stream called the Volp flows through it, and it has galleries running in all directions with some splendid drawings. In one of its upper storeys there is the famous 'clay bisons', a carving which dates from the Magdalenian period, about two feet long. And there are the marks of human hands and footprints of cave-bears. The Trois-Frères was discovered in 1914 and contains a very striking drawing of a witch-doctor, among other things."

The sun was very hot and I was longing for the coolness of the caves. We were now heading for Foix, but we stopped shortly before reaching the town to visit the underground river at Labouiche.

Here we met two friends of Monsieur Casteret, Joseph Delteil and Mademoiselle Annie Cazenave. Annie is a native of Ariège. Although still very young she is already established as an archivist and at the time was studying twelfth-century murals in the local churches. She goes in for pot-holing as a hobby.

As for Joseph Delteil, he and Monsieur Casteret had become acquainted on this very spot twenty-three years before, and since then had often teamed up together and explored a great many caves and pot-holes. For me he will always be associated with Labouiche. It was wonderful to hear him talk about it, because to some extent he has made the river his own. It was there that he fell incurably in love with speleology.

"The river has been partly cleared and built up," said Monsieur Casteret. "It was a good thing to do because it's a great tourist attraction, being conveniently situated on the road to Foix and containing some wonderful stalactites. One travels along it by boat, which will be very restful, and we shall have the honour of being personally conducted by Delteil."

We had the further honour of being received by the head guide, who for my sake opened the glass case containing the relief model of the river. I was able to follow its outlines with my finger while the others described it to me in detail.

"I think it would be better," said Delteil, "if we went the opposite way to the one taken by ordinary visitors. We shall then be follow-ing Martel's route. He was the first person to enter Labouiche."

So, like the explorer E. A. Martel in 1908, we went on to the River Fajal, which goes underground not far from there, after wind-ing for a long way through woods and meadows. We got into a big, flat-bottomed boat and were borne silently into the tunnel.

"Would you like to steer?" Delteil asked me. "It's very simple. All you have to do is keep a hand on the guide-rail let into the wall or ceiling and the boat will take care of itself."

"How funny it feels! You'd think the rail was moving and the boat was standing still!"

Presently we came to the junction of the Fajal and the Labouiche, and here the tunnel widened considerably. We turned into the Labouiche and went upstream towards its source. The stream was very gentle and smooth-flowing, but of course the boat now had to be pulled along, and so Annie and Delteil took over.

I sat with folded arms, in the attitude I prefer when I am listening or thinking. I was remembering a children's book I had read in which there was a description of an underground river which I felt sure must be this one, because I seemed to recognise it. It was particularly kind of Monsieur Casteret to have brought me here, because, as I knew he preferred to avoid caves that have been done up for tourists.

My companions must have thought me very uncommunicative. I made no attempt to talk, because silence seems to me essential underground. I withdrew into myself, feeling the motion of the boat while I thought of Martel travelling along that same tunnel in 1908, alone, but happy, I was sure, in his small, ill-lit canoe. The next year he had returned with a party of eight, in five boats, and they had gone much farther, despite several shipwrecks. But the river went farther still. A Dr. Cremadells, from Foix, one of the members of Martel's expedition, had returned to it later, but it still kept its secret. No one knew its source.

"Are there any prehistoric remains?" I asked.

"Yes, a number have been found in a dry cave above the Fajal, in particular a picture of a lion engraved on a piece of stone, which is very rare."

""What about vegetation?"

"There's very little in the caves, but one comes across moss and fern in places where there's light, near the electric bulbs."

"Do you mean that the tunnel isn't lighted everywhere?"

"No. At this moment we're in darkness. It's done on purpose, to give tourists a thrill . . . Better keep your head down. The roof's low just here."

Monsieur Casteret said: "I found it very impressive when I came here alone in a small canoe in 1937. Some parts of the tunnel are low and dark, but others are lofty and filled with natural decorations which make one think of cathedrals and bell-towers and minarets . . . Reach out and touch that drapery on your right. Its folds are very elegant."

Further on the stream spread out into small bays and creeks, and there were beaches, long banks running down to the water. There were even bones, and I wondered who had brought them there.

"Oh, look at the wonderful stalactites!" exclaimed Annie.

"I've got one," I said.

I had broken off a small one in passing. There was a general laugh, and I realised, too late, that I should not have done it. If every visitor broke one off! . . . But Monsieur Casteret only said: "Sometimes they splinter like glass. Be careful you don't cut yourself."

We passed other boats, and ourselves changed boats several times. We were making now for the waterfall.

"On our left," said Delteil, "there's a small tributary. Can you hear its fall? It drops into a deep, cold, turbulent pool. That's where Casteret and I had lunch in 1937, the day after his solo trip."

"Did you go ashore and picnic on a beach?"

"There aren't any. The pool's surrounded by sheer walls. One has to be very careful in an inflatable boat, or it may be punctured by sharp concretions."

"So you had your meal afloat. I hope you didn't drop it in the water."

"No fear! It was the only meal we had that day!"

"I must say," said Monsieur Casteret, "that considering it was his first trip underground Delteil did very well. He insisted on drinking out of the bottle, and what with his helmet and the position we were in the effect was so comical that he nearly choked through swallowing the wrong way."

"And what happens above the fall?"

"We expected to find a fossilised level higher up, because all the subterranean rivers started by flowing above ground and gradually sank and were covered over. And when we got up there, after a lot of difficult climbing, we eventually came to it."

"What's it like?"

"It varies a great deal. There are some very narrow channels, either limestone or clay, and some enormous chambers with huge stalactites and stalagmites. We christened one of these Phoebus, after the famous Comte de Foix. Then there are two chasms leading to a lower level, and they end in a most beautiful grotto with green water of a colour we'd never seen before."

"But what becomes of the river?"

"You have to go through a very sticky clay corridor and you reach it again at the foot of another fall. Higher up there's an impassable sump. In 1955 a Franco-British party tried to get through it with underwater equipment, but it goes too deep and it's too long. So there are about six miles of the river which are unexplored."

We now headed for the exit, after visiting a magnificent chamber adorned with a no less splendid cluster of stalagmites which I examined with my hands under the guidance of my companions. In one corner I found a burst of crystal drapery that would have done very well for my collection, but—"We haven't broken any off, Delteil," said Monsieur Casteret hastily, being now aware of my predatory habits.

"It was in this cavern," said Delteil, "that the Bishop of Pamiers celebrated Mass in 1955, for the benefit of the members of the Franco-British team. There were a great many tourists there as well. Then the bishop went upstream in a boat to bless the frogmen who were going to try to get through the sump. It was very moving."

We regretfully left the coolness of the cave for the heat outside. It was Annie who opened the grille.

"I know the combination of the padlock," she said.

I heard a series of clicks while she muttered figures under her breath.

"How do you do it?" I asked, intrigued.

She told me what the combination was and how it was done. The gate opened and we passed through. Annie stayed behind, since she knew how to shut it . . .

I was making desperate and unsuccessful efforts not to laugh, and Monsieur Casteret asked me what the joke was. I did not answer. In any case there was now a silence while the others wondered what Annie was doing. It seemed that she was looking for something. Delteil went to her assistance while I laughed to myself.

"I've lost the padlock," she said finally.

"But you can't have! You had it in your hand a minute ago!"

"Well, I haven't got it now."

I had taken it. Without saying anything I handed it to Monsieur Casteret, who laughed in his turn and restored it to her.

"Annie's always making us laugh! First she gives away the secret of the combination and then she loses the padlock." He added in a low voice, for my benefit: "She's still at it. She's closing the grille with herself on the inside!"

It was in this happy spirit that we took leave of Labouiche, after signing the visitor's book.

5

The Bedeilhac Cave, Ariège

THE talk as we drove along the Dauphine was always interesting— how could it be otherwise in the company of Monsieur Casteret? I made a great many notes about the caves in the region, and he thought braille a very practical system of writing because I was not affected by the swaying and vibration of the car.

After a pleasant meal at Foix, the town with three fortified keeps, we passed under the imposing vault of the Bedeilhac cave. Imposing is not too large a word, for the entrance is seventy yards wide.

Annie Cazenave and Joseph Delteil joined us there, having come in another car, and we all put on our canvas overalls and helmets again. Because of the huge dimensions and unusual lay-out of the cave, light penetrates a long way inside it, and so we were able to drive in and park the cars under the roof, where there is ample space.

"We're in a vast, concreted porch," Monsieur Casteret explained to me. "It was done during the last war by the Germans, who were planning to build an aircraft factory here."

"But is the whole cave concreted?"

"No, don't be alarmed, they hadn't time. But unfortunately their tidying-up operations had already destroyed a number of pre-historic sites."

Monsieur Casteret went on to tell me that the first underground television broadcast had been made from this cave, and a live one at that. The technicians had had to overcome great difficulties in setting up their transformers and cameras, but it had been a success.

We walked along that impressive natural cathedral where a solitude exists that is unknown to the outside world. The concrete floor gave place to earth, at first clay with sandy patches, littered with boulders but easy to walk along. This hall was about half a mile long and very lofty; we counted and found that it was eighty paces wide.

"Over on the left," said Delteil, pointing his torch at the wall, "is the narrow tunnel we had to crawl out of for the television performance. Something went wrong with one of the cameras, and they kept us waiting so long that I fell asleep lying on my stomach in the mud."

Diggings at the end of the cave had uncovered human remains and a variety of objects dating from the Musterian period.

"And here," said Monsieur Casteret, "is a huge stalagmitic monument—the Fountain! Not much water has come out of it this year because of the drought. This is where we were grouped together to speak into the microphone during the broadcast."

I walked round and then climbed up the stalagmite, and took a pebble as a souvenir from the hollow bowl, like a font, at the top.

"The cave has always been known," continued Monsieur Casteret, "because of its position and extraordinary size. There are drawings dating from a number of periods, Aurignacian, Magdalenian and later. But unfortunately most of the colouring has faded, particularly in the case of the four bisons at the end."

Moving at random I touched majestic columns, a forest of huge natural pillars. I had not believed that such vast formations could exist. Some were as much as forty feet in circumference. There were also complicated drapery-patterns covered with a very white greasy substance, a form of calcite, generally known by its German name of Mondmilch (moon-milk). I tasted it out of curiosity. It had a musty flavour that was not at all unpleasant.

My companions called to me to come and examine "Roland's Tomb". This was an enormous column, some thirty-five feet long and eighteen in diameter, lying on the ground like a fallen tree. Just as in the cross-cut of a tree one can count the rings of growth formed by the years, so here, on this uprooted column, one could feel the limestone accretions formed by the millennia. It seemed unbelievable that so vast an object could have been created simply by drops of water—to be overthrown in the end by who can say what cataclysm! . . .

Since the natural groining of its surface was now horizontal it afforded excellent hand- and footholds, and I took advantage of these to climb up its side. It was a long time since I had had such a comfortable climb. Monsieur Casteret joined me and we walked up and down it, eighteen feet above ground, while Annie and Delteil looked on.

After negotiating a number of passageways so low that we had to go on all fours, keeping our heads down, we reached the end of the cave-system, a vast chamber filled with columns and stalagmites of all sizes. There was even a little rotunda formed of an infinite number of concretions and small columns, but with room inside it for both Annie and me. There were mysterious niches and recesses everywhere, where one was tempted to remain, to meditate or pray.

As we went along the bed of a dry stream I studied in its fossil banks the successive alluvial layers deposited through the ages, rather like a *mille-feuille* pastry. Here we were walking on a floor of alluvial silt with few obstacles. It was very different from Riousec, where one never came in direct contact with the earth, so covered was it by the tons of rock fallen from the roof.

Following the general custom, we paused for a little while at the end of the cave before starting back. It was hard to imagine the religious and domestic events which must have occurred in this place, so long ago . . . But it was pleasant to think of them in silence, with the lamps out.

Monsieur Casteret told us a little story of something that had happened at Labastide a few weeks previously.

"I was with a couple of visitors who wanted to see the Roaring Lion cavern," he said. "They had a two-months-old baby which they couldn't leave outside, but the young mother was terribly anxious to visit the cave. So we wrapped the baby up and put it in a sort of carry-cot like the Eskimos use, and passed it through the bars of the grille. It was very well behaved. We carried it through the halls and galleries, and we reached the terminal chamber just in time for its next feed. So the mother, quite simply, put it to her breast. I said, 'It must be at least twenty thousand years since anything of the kind has happened here!' Anyway, that is certainly one pot-holer who won't remember his first cave!"

Most of the day had been spent underground and it was high time for us to be getting back to Saint-Gaudens, sixty miles distant. I was not to have the delight of touching the little bison of Bedeilhac, a masterpiece of prehistoric sculpture.

"Cheer up," said Monsieur Casteret, giving me rather doubtful consolation. "It's so fragile that I shouldn't have allowed you to touch it."

Annie and Delteil talked about branches of the cave which lack of time had prevented us from exploring—the Vidal Gallery, the Gallery of Winds, and another where in 1958 Raymonde Casteret and Georges Lepineux had given a masterly display of climbing for television.

The party broke up, promising to meet again to visit other caves, and we took cordial leave of one another in the warm summer evening, abandoning Bedeilhac to the solitude of the mountains overshadowing it. We also said a last goodbye to the ruined Château de Calames before driving through the village of Saurat and up the long, rising road to the Col de Port, with an empty expanse of bracken on either side.

Beyond the Col we came down by a series of great bends amid green meadows to the little town of Massat, where the women still wear the traditional black costume, and which contains a Magdalenian cave decorated with drawings of horse and ibex.

That morning we had had the good fortune to hear crickets and to drive past the Massif de Soudour where, very high up, there is the Cave of Pradières, which is so dear to me. This evening we drove through a region of flowering thorn, lush meadows and happy, smiling villages, real old-world villages which still possess very old crosses.

As the day ended we came in sight of Mont Vallier, which Monsieur Casteret described to me. It is nearly 10,000 feet and is known locally as the Giant of the Pyrenees, so formidable are its lofty, limestone faces, and so difficult to climb. We had emerged from the underground world and now the peaks were calling to us! How wonderful to be alive, with so much to be explored! And tomorrow was another day.

6

The Tignahustes Cave, Hautes-Pyrénées

I SAT in Monsieur Casteret's study, at Mourlon, thinking of all the caves I would like to visit.

There was Montespan, which contains the oldest statues in the world, discovered by Monsieur Casteret in 1923; Espassos, "the apotheosis of chasms"; Aldène, where five human footprints twenty-five thousand years old were discovered in an admirable state of preservation; the Casteret ice-cave, discovered and explored in 1926 by the famous family whose name it bears; the five Isard caves. These last, situated on the Spanish side of Mount Marboré, are the highest caves in the world. There were the caves of Mas d'Azil, Lherm Sabat, Enlène, Niaux, Lombrives, le Portel and many others.

Every cave has a character of its own, and the big room in which I sat was full of souvenirs of them, and of their life. A cave-explorer in the heart of a cavern thinks of light, but in a room bathed in light he longs for the darkness underground.

We decided that today we would enter the silence of the Tigna-hustes Cave, to observe and meditate. But before setting out for that modest and little-known cave, situated not far from Montréjeau at the confluence of the Rivers Neste and Garonne, I leaned once more on the window-ledge looking towards the Pyrenees which I could not see but already loved so dearly, in the tranquil atmosphere of the study.

It was filled with books, portraits and explorer's gear: helmets, torches, lamps, rolls of very fine "electron" ladder, ice-axes, climbing irons, pegs for driving into rock and ice, a chisel and mallet for widening holes in stalagmite formations, a block and tackle for use with ladders, a compass, and a thousand other things each more fascinating than the last because of the underground adventures they evoked.

I should have liked to spend hours in that big, sunny room where so many inspiring books have been written. I had an especial esteem for the two water-worn wooden rungs of the ladder used by the great explorer, Martel, in 1899, in the Aven de Grand-Gérin (Vaucluse). They were found in 1956, fifty-seven years later, by Rover Scouts from Aix-en-Provence.

The bookcase was adorned with two magnificent gipsum stalactites from the Cigalère cave. There was also a piece of red sandstone from the Raymonde pit, two flint arrowheads from the Sahara and a piece of fossilised wood as heavy as stone. There was a case of pottery dating from various periods and a large, very rare, fulgurite found at Labastide. This was a piece of rock struck by lightning, which made it look like glass. The entrance to a cave can be dangerous in a thunderstorm.

Monsieur Casteret had given me a number of animals' skulls to touch, Pyrenean bears, badgers, martens, squirrels, etc., and even— I was very moved—the tiny cranium of a bat. He has written wonderfully about bats in his books. They are harmless, useful little creatures, and highly intelligent. Monsieur Casteret has spent years observing and studying them, and I knew he would have a great deal to tell me about them on today's outing, because the Tigna-hustes Cave, where he was taking me, was once the home of bats.

Among the many things in that room which I vividly remember I must mention the splendid relief-model of the Pyrenees made by Monsieur Casteret. Small pins inserted in the Massif de la Maladetta indicated the sources and resurgence of the River Garonne, as well as other chasms.

And now I stood at the window with the Pyrenees in front of me. How could I fail to dream? Over to the right was the Massif de Lourdes with the Pic du Midi.

But Lourdes is first and foremost the Miraculous Grotto where the greatest of all Mothers did not disdain to appear to a little girl from our country, very poor, simple and innocent.

In one sense, a cave like any other, which Monsieur Casteret was asked to explore in 1940, to see what could be done to prevent the seepage of water after heavy rainfalls, which was damaging the altar. And at the same time a cave like no other, where people go to drink and bathe in the water of the Miraculous Spring which the Virgin caused to flow on 25th February, 1858.

By a natural association of ideas I thought also of the humble cave in Bethlehem, and all the others frequented by the Holy Family during their time on earth.

Returning to the Pyrenees I pictured the great peaks of the frontier crest—the Port de Vanasque, the Nethou, and further distant, to my left, the peaks of Ariège with their famous caves. Closer at hand were woods and fields and the town of Saint-Gaudens with its carillon of twenty bells whose joyous peal I had come to know.

But now it was two o'clock and time to go. Without regret I abandoned day-dreaming for the reality of underground, where, in Monsieur Casteret's words, "More than elsewhere there exists, rich in solemnity and unassailable majesty, an element of wonder and the spirit. Here mystery creates a climate eminently favourable to escape from material things and communication with a Divine Presence. Here it is always possible to talk intimately with God. It is the appeal of silence and solitude which, in every age, has moved and attracted certain men, and impelled them to live in caves . . ."

In order to reach the small, overhung entrance of the Grotte des Tignahustes we had to force our way through a thick undergrowth of shrub and thorn that exhaled a heady scent, and then climb a very steep bank, gripping the branches of wild hazel and cherry trees. When at last we reached the tiny opening we sat down to get our breath.

"I have spent whole nights here alone," Monsieur Casteret said, "in an attempt to learn something about the life of bats, especially the big, migratory species known as murines. The small bats one finds around human habitations do not migrate. It is only the larger kinds, with a wingspan of perhaps eighteen inches, which set out like the swallows to winter in the South."

"How long do they stay in these parts?"

"About six months, from March to September. They go out every night at the same time to forage. They feed on cockchafers, moths, mosquitoes, midges, crickets and other things."

"And they always come back to the same cave?"

"Oh, yes, always. They lived here for centuries. They have a remarkable sense of direction and a wonderful gift of flight. In that respect they're far superior to most birds. Their normal flying speed is nearly twenty miles an hour, and on their oversea migrations they reach nearly forty."

"That's extraordinary."

"Bats are descended from a zoological species belonging to the Secondary Period. There are twenty-five different kinds in France."

"But how exactly do they steer themselves?"

"It's as though they had a small compass in their head, or a radar. They're guided by ultra-sound, pitched beyond the range that we can hear, and atmospheric and electrical phenomena. When they're in a cave and the weather's bad outside they know this and don't attempt to leave it, because they know in advance that there will be no food to be found. We're still learning about them. It exasperates me when I hear of people being terrified of them, and hunting and killing them. They really aren't as repellent as all that! But you need to study them to realise what they're capable of."

"They have a sixth sense!" I said, almost overcome with emotion. "The same sixth sense that is attributed to us blind people. They really possess it, and in a wonderful degree. They're lucky. Yes, they're very lucky indeed!"

"It is believed that this extra faculty is situated in the semicircular channels in their ears. In fact, they perceive objects at a distance by 'hearing' them, so to speak. They're also helped by the extreme sensitivity of their wing-membrane."

I was fascinated by all that Monsieur Casteret had to tell me as we sat outside the Grotte des Tignahustes, which means the Cave of Bats.

Certainly the bats are superior to humans in some respects. A blind person who is accustomed to getting about alone—in the streets, for instance—can also, with long practice, perceive objects at a distance—sometimes, although not always. But what he cannot perceive is a downward step or hollow, and this has been the cause of many accidents.

Every now and then we are told in the newspapers or on the radio that a portable radar equipment for the blind has been devised. Splendid, provided it can detect gaps as well as solid bodies! But the announcer nearly always adds, "The apparatus is still a little too bulky for everyday use . . ." No doubt the price is equally bulky! It's a pity we aren't bats.

I crawled in on hands and knees behind Monsieur Casteret and again smelt the familiar cavern smell and heard the sound of dropping water. I had a wildly joyous feeling at finding myself back in that subterranean world of which my life elsewhere can never efface the memory. A downward slope brought us to a small chamber, and then, still in single file, we climbed up a narrow tunnel which brought us to a second chamber similar to the first.

"This is where I came to catch bats," said Monsieur Casteret. "Here's a bit of the long wooden pole I used."

"How did you go about it?"

"I fixed a sort of fishing net on the end of the pole and ran it along the rows of bats hanging from the roof. I caught two hundred and twenty-five on my first visit. I ringed them, like one does birds, and took them home with me and then let them go. Later I took them much greater distances, several hundred miles. They always came back here. I found my ringed specimens when I came to look for them."

"How many bats were there in this cave? I say 'were' because I imagine your visits must have driven them away."

"Yes, that did happen. There must have been nearly a thousand, but in the end they moved elsewhere so as not to be disturbed. I don't know where they went, but it was certainly somewhere less accessible than here."

We were walking on a small hill of droppings which filled the entire centre of the cave and proved that bats must have lived in it for many centuries. The chamber was at least twenty yards across.

"Do bats live a long time?"

"Undoubtedly. In 1960 I found one in the Labastide cave which I'd ringed in 1936. It was fully-grown when I ringed it, but the teeth still showed no sign of wear. The system of ringing is very interesting. By 1950 there were sixty-five of us doing it in France . . . I'm looking to see if there's a skeleton of a bat anywhere."

"Oh," I exclaimed, "I should so love to have one like the one you let me examine in your showcase."

"I can't find one. The murine has a big head and a pointed snout, long ears and a rough pelt. Its blood temperature is thirty-seven degrees, but during the period of somnolence, in winter, this falls to the temperature of the surrounding air."

"I have read," I said, "that the Mochicas, a pre-Inca race in Peru, worshipped bats. It's nice to think, isn't it, that at least one people held them to be sacred because of their especial gifts."

Although I had thought the cave a small one it contained a number of curiosities, pointed out to me by Monsieur Casteret, which filled me with wonder and delight.

"I'm going to take you down to a lower floor," he said, "because here we're in a hydrogeological cave. A stream once flowed through it."

"Is the descent difficult?"

"No. I'll go first. Mind your head."

Monsieur Casteret climbed quickly down and then gave me instructions for following him.

"This is how it is. I can't do anything to secure you because I'm below and anyway we haven't brought a rope. There aren't many footholds and its slippery. I would advise you to come down backwards. As soon as your feet come within my reach I'll find holds for them."

It was only a small descent, but I knew that underground one has to be careful. However, since Monsieur Casteret said it was all right I had to make the attempt. I went backwards on hands and knees until I reached the opening, but then I lay flat on my stomach and did not move.

"What's happened?" asked Monsieur Casteret, who could only see my feet by the light of his lamp.

"Nothing's happened. I'm stuck and I'm afraid to go any further."

"But why? There's a good hold only a few inches below your left foot."

"Even a few inches is too much. If I move at all I shall start slipping."

"Isn't there any projection you can hold on to on your left?"

"Yes, there is, but I don't feel safe. I'm afraid I shall lose my grip."

"Well, in that case you'd better go back. I can't see your hand-holds from here and so I've no way of guiding you."

I felt two hands vigorously thrusting my feet forward. But then I realised that it was no easier for me to go up than to go down. I had to make up my mind. If I didn't go down I should always regret it.

"I'm coming down!" I said.

I did so finally, rejoining my companion in the light of the acetylene lamp after having given a very poor demonstration of my climbing ability. What must he think of me? But I did not really care, because I was happy to find that my love of adventure had been stronger than the fear of a void that sometimes overtakes me at the most unexpected moments.

We examined this lower floor which had been formed by a lofty crack in the limestone formation, and I was the more pleased with it since it gave access to a pit . . . Then, after collecting a stalactite, we climbed up again without trouble.

"There's another part of this cave I'd like to show you," said Monsieur Casteret. "But it means climbing. It's nearly all clay and there are spiders."

"Never mind. Let's go!"

This time I went first along the tunnel. I knew that there were no large extensions of the Tignahustes cave, but still I found it very thrilling.

"I can feel a slight draught," I said, stopping suddenly. "Don't you think it may mean that there's an extension?"

"No,· there isn't one. But you may have felt a puff of warm air from outside, because round about here there's a small hole leading to the surface."

"But the air wasn't warm. And now I can't feel it any more."

"Then it was probably me. I must have set up a stir by making a sudden movement. One's so sensitive to everything underground that one tends to get things out of proportion."

"Well, now I really can feel an opening on my left. Where does it lead to?"

"Nowhere. I explored it years ago. It's just a cat-hole about twenty yards long that doesn't get anywhere."

"Can I try it? But I can't even get in. My shoulders are too wide."

"Well, I managed, and you're slimmer than I am."

"I'm sure I can't do it. And anyway, would I be able to get out, wriggling backwards?"

"You haven't got the trick yet. It comes with practice. There's a way of placing one's arms and shoulders—"

"Ah, now I know! I've found out how to do it. If I lie a bit on my side with my left shoulder on the ground I ought to be able to get in."

"Yes, but it's getting late. I'm afraid, Colette, it's time for us to be going back to Saint-Gaudens."

Crawling on hands and knees along the low tunnel we made our way out of the cave.

The intense brightness and warmth of the sunshine outside came as a surprise to us. Our clothes were muddy but we were in the highest spirits, and, as was proper, the expedition ended in a burst of laughter.

"When I think," said Monsieur Casteret, "that you wanted to force your way along a cat-hole with your helmet and pockets full of pebbles!"

Indeed, I was very innocent and inexperienced. I laughed wholeheartedly, thinking how comical I must have seemed.

The reader of these lines on the Cave of Bats will perhaps spare a grateful thought for Clement Ader, who was inspired by a bat in the construction of his little aeroplane. And we may conclude with the following passage from the writings of Monsieur Casteret:

"Who knows but that someday, in the silence of a laboratory or the heart of a cave, a biologist will penetrate the secret of the highly-developed senses of those pariahs of creation, the bats? Who knows but that they will someday furnish the basis of a discovery capable of enabling the deaf to hear, and perhaps of restoring sight to the blind, or at least of alleviating their disability? . . . May the harmless and useful bats, so unjustly feared and defamed, one day earn the gratitude of the afflicted by inspiring the labours of some scientist who will become the Father of the Blind, just as Clement Ader, in building his aeroplane, 'The Bat', became the Father of Aviation."

7

Night in Solitude

O<small>N</small> 30th August we went to the Caverne de Gargas, but it was not to be a visit like the others.

From the day of my arrival Monsieur Casteret had sought, by taking me to caves of different kinds, and by gradually increasing their difficulty, to give me a precise idea of speleology and above all to teach me to love the subterranean world. Speleology is more than a pastime, because in practising it one gains constantly in spiritual strength. To be a true cave-explorer one needs to have lived underground, to have come in intimate contact with those rocks that are so living, so compelling in their mystery; one must not be afraid of them. It seems to me that if one loves anyone or anything one must never be afraid, or there can be no real friendship or truth. Cave-explorers love risk and effort; above all they seek to learn, to know and to discover. But scientific curiosity must always be accompanied by courage.

For a very long time I had wanted to spend a night alone in a cave, and this called for the fulfilment of a great many conditions. However it seemed to me, after our visit to the Grotte des Tignahustes, that the time had come to broach the idea to Monsieur Casteret. He seemed rather taken aback, and this surprised me.

"You know," he said, "there are many experienced speleologists who wouldn't spend a night underground for anything on earth. I must say I hadn't expected this. And you want to do it tomorrow!"

"I've really no choice, because I'm leaving so soon."

"Just so. That is why we had hoped that you would spend a quiet family evening with us."

At least he had not said no, which was hopeful; but I knew that I should have to be very persuasive if I was to overcome all the objections he was certain to raise. We discussed it for a long time, and eventually he gave way. We decided upon the Caverne de Gargas.

We were welcomed at Gargas by Monsieur Louron, who is the present tenant of the cave. It is large and of great prehistoric interest, but only its lower part is open to the public.

We first entered the great Hall of the Bear, on the left hand wall of which there are strange imprints—those of hands with finger-joints missing.

"The prints are red or black," said Monsieur Casteret. "The mutilations indicate sacrificial offerings of the kind practised by certain prehistoric tribes in their magic or religious ceremonies. The prints are scattered all over the wall, and there can be no doubt of their authenticity because in places they are covered over with a very thin limestone crust . . . And here on the right there are two incised drawings which you can feel—a bovine head and the head of a horse."

We went on into a vast, empty gallery in which there were several right-angle turns. The floor was rather like a chessboard, pitted with small hollows in which water collected during the rainy season. The gallery was awe-inspiring, seeming to me even more silent than most, and filled with brooding mystery. And this was where I was to spend the night!

"There's a small recess here with a very fine imprint of a hand. But it isn't incised, unfortunately, so you won't be able to feel it."

"How old are these imprints estimated to be?"

"Between twenty and thirty thousand years. At the far end of the gallery there's a place known as the 'Oubliette' which I want to show you. Some very interesting excavations have been carried out there."

"That must be where the things came from that were in the showcase outside, which the guide so kindly opened for me before we entered the cave."

"Yes. They found bones of bears, hyenas, wolves, bison and horses, also teeth and various other things."

We made our way along a deep trench cut in the clay. Here and there I noted small patches of delicate moss and tiny fern.

"There's an insect on the wall, a sort of moth, let's see if you can catch it," said Monsieur Casteret, and took my hand to guide it. He did not know that I have a horror of insects. Although it repelled me. I said nothing, since it was a cave insect and in any case very small. I forced myself to touch it.

On the right of the trench there was an intriguing branch-passage full of mysterious bends. We went along it.

"All the periods are represented here—pre-Aurignacian, Magdalenian, Early Christian, Middle Ages. Here's an incised drawing of an ibex."

"When I was a girl-guide I chose an ibex for my patrol-emblem. What other pictures are there?"

"Various heads, and the remains of a horse, of which one can only see the hooves. There are also some very ancient imprints of hands deeply impressed in the soft clay and gradually covered with a stalagmitic layer."

"This is a beautiful hand!"

"Yes, and remarkably well-preserved. You're lucky. Your slender fingers exactly fit the mould."

It was true that I was lucky, and I found the experience as deeply moving as when, at Labastide, I had touched the head of the Roaring Lion. The fingers of my left hand fitted the imprint as though I had made it myself. Thirty thousand years separating this gesture of two hands! . . . Kneeling by the wall we remained silent, assailed by too many questions. Only a solemn silence could answer them; at least it did not profane those treasures come to us from so long ago.

"At the end of this passage," said Monsieur Casteret, "there's a 'Chrisma' carved by early Christians—a Cross with the Alpha and Omega."

There were also two crossbows certainly dating from the Middle Ages.

"This would be an excellent place for you to spend the night," said Monsieur Casteret. "It's small and the ceiling's low. You wouldn't be cold."

"No," I said. "Not here."

"Why not?"

"I want an unknown place, somewhere unexplored. There are too many memories here, too much magic and mystery. It's too overwhelming. I should like to come here to meditate, because it's hard to tear oneself away. But to stay here for a long time would be more than I could bear. There's so much intensity, such a concentration of forces and age-old lives . . . I'd like to come back here, if I may."

One has to impose limits on the hunger for experience, not go too fast, let oneself become gradually acclimatised, even when one is sure of oneself. One needs to repeat constantly, "I will come back later." This is not weakness or fear or laziness, but self-discipline.

We continued along the trench, which presently brought us to the Grotte Supérieure. On the left of this hall is the famous stalactite formation known as the "Organ of Gargas". The stalactites possess an extraordinary resonance, and by the use of a small hammer fixed to a long pole one can play a tune on them as on a xylophone. But I was not privileged to hear this carillon. There have been so many performances that some of the stalactites are now cracked and broken.

There were also prehistoric stippled designs on the walls which no one has been able to interpret.

"Here's a bone of a horse, Colette, for you to add to your collection," said Monsieur Casteret. "And now, if you like, we'll climb to the upper floor of the cave, which I discovered and explored in 1937."

"Shall we have to use a ladder?"

"I'm not sure. I'll go first and haul up our rucksacks with the rope."

Moving with extreme care, my companion reached the top of an old and very ricketty flight of wooden steps. I was left in darkness somewhere near their foot, propped against a damp wall. It was a little sinister. I touched some interesting limestone formations while I waited for orders.

"Good, I've got the rucksacks up. Now it's your turn. Describe your exact position to me so that I can tell you what to do, because I can't see you from here."

"Well, I've got a wall on my right and I'm facing downhill."

"Move a little to your left and then forward. You'll find the steps and the rope hanging. All right?"

"I can't find the rope." I floundered about for a few moments. "Ah, now I've got it!"

"Good. Tie it round you and come up gently."

I climbed gingerly up the rotting, slippery steps, taking care not to put both feet on one at the same time. It was a tricky business, but better than standing at the bottom doing nothing. Then we continued along a downward-sloping gallery, in which there were a number of projections and sharp changes of level. There were prickly stalactites which I liked; some made me think of small roses.

"Here's a steep bit. I'll go ahead and you can pass the lamps down to me."

I moved slowly forward with great care so as not to drop the lamps, and after passing them one at a time to my companion I joined him by sliding down with my rucksack. We then walked in single file along a trench a hundred yards long which brought us to the great Norbert Casteret chamber.

"Yes, I came here in 1937, but the trench wasn't dug then. I had to crawl along a *laminoir*, a sort of lateral fissure, with a mass of small pillars and concretions. This chamber gives access to two shafts. But it's getting late. We must have something to eat and then find a place for you to spend the night."

We went back along the trench and then into a *laminoir* of the kind he had mentioned, which might be called a "flat", a very low but wide passageway along which we had to crawl for ten minutes —my first long crawl. Monsieur Casteret led the way. I don't know how he managed not to lose himself in that labyrinth. He held the two lamps and pushed his rucksack in front of him. Every now and then I touched the soles of his boots to make sure I was going the right way. I was flat on my stomach, using knees and elbows to get myself along; but the whole body has to work in that kind of operation, which is extremely tiring—and in addition I was dragging my rucksack behind me.

"Colette, here's a cat-hole. Are you following closely?"

"Yes."

I couldn't lift my head or get up on hands and knees. The stalactites hanging from the roof pricked my back, and I touched some beautiful columns in passing. We negotiated two more holes, a muddy tunnel and a number of bends, crawling all the way. Mercifully my rucksack on its rope did not give me too much trouble.

I broke off a long, hollow stalactite like a stick of macaroni, but it was very fragile and crumpled in my hand.

I was very happy, filled with a delight resembling that which one feels in the mountains as one draws near a great summit; but here it was intensified because the obstacles were ten times greater.

"The cave-explorer, the crawler, more than any other person experiences the particular joy of discovery and adventure, the intoxicating sense of entering places where no one has set foot since the beginning of the world."

Monsieur Casteret's words, running through my mind, were very applicable to me at that moment. He was the only person to have explored that upper part of the cave. It was rather as though he were taking me to the first opening night of a play.

The roof became a little higher, just enough for us to be able to sit down.

"But we can't go any further," said Monsieur Casteret, "without climbing down into the pit just ahead of us, and that will have to be postponed to our next visit. I think it's time for dinner, don't you?"

"I'm ravenous!"

"Good."

The ceiling of our odd dining-room was more or less horizontal, but the floor sloped. We sat down in the lowest part and examined the contents of our rucksacks.

"I can positively offer you a paper napkin," said Monsieur Casteret, "which is unheard-of luxury underground. And there's sausage. And here's a little knife which you can keep as a souvenir. It's rather charmingly old-fashioned and I've had it a long time."

I had seen the knife before, having used it at Riousec. It had a craved bone handle inlaid with mother-of-pearl. I was moved to think of the many subterranean excursions on which it must have served.

We ate in silence, seated side by side in that lost corner in the entrails of the the earth. It was a quarter to nine and I knew that we should soon be separating. There was something splendid in that simplicity, something not easy to explain, one has to have lived it to understand.

Without saying very much we arranged my bed in the most suitable spot—a groundsheet, a sleeping-bag and, for a pillow, the coil of rope wrapped in my overalls; all this on the sloping floor, half clay and half stalagmite. The only inconvenience, a trifling one, was that I could not sit upright, the distance from floor to ceiling being only about two feet.

"Well," said Monsieur Casteret, "I think that's everything. I'm leaving you the roll of ladder, which we haven't used, the rucksack with supplies, the flask of orangeade, the acetylene lamp and an electric safety-torch. Oh, I forgot, there are some pears, but I'm afraid they suffered rather badly while we were crawling through the 'flat'."

"I'm sure I'm going to be beautifully comfortable."

"Here's a whistle, in case you want to amuse yourself during the night. And here are matches for the lamp. You must be careful to keep them in a dry place."

I put the lanyard of the whistle round my neck and the box of matches in my pyjama-pocket. We were both behaving as naturally as possible, although we both felt that we were living through a solemn experience. I would have liked to prolong those minutes of intensity and truth.

"You won't move away from this spot, will you?"

"No, I promise."

"When I get here, tomorrow morning, I'll blow my whistle and then you'll know it isn't a bear. There are a lot of bears' bones about, particularly on the slope leading to the chasm."

"I don't hear much water dropping."

"No, the roof's pretty dry. No risk of you getting a cold shower, which is lucky . . . And now, if you like, we'll repeat the prayer we say every evening at home."

So, like early Christians in the catacombs, two huddled speleologists—huddled because there was not room to kneel upright—prayed to the Creator and the Mother of the World . . . It was simple, intimate and beautiful, and our two acetylene lamps kept soft vigil over us . . . "Our Lady of Chasms, pray for us . . ."

"Shall I go now?"

"Yes,"

"Well, then, goodnight, Colette, and au revoir. I shall be back at six tomorrow morning."

Now we were perfectly at ease. We shook hands and Monsieur Casteret vanished into the "flat", on his way back to his home at Saint-Gaudens, a short drive by car. He had left me the rosary which he always carried in his pocket. I heard his movements, as he wriggled through the "flat", for exactly seven minutes.

Then nothing. I was alone in the Gargas cave.

Nine hours of absolute solitude. Would they be long or short? I took off my dark glasses and put them in the upturned helmet beside me, also a stylus and pad, in case I wanted to write in braille during the night. The helmet had belonged to Madame Casteret, that great explorer of whom it was said that she "did difficult things easily". I hoped that on this, my first night underground, I would not be unworthy of her, I who was in some sort her spiritual daughter in speleology. She had explored more than three hundred caves and was remembered with affection by everyone who had met her. I had never known her, but I admired her intensely and felt almost unworthy to have worn her helmet on six expeditions, although I was sure it had brought me luck.

I put out the acetylene lamp and snuggled down. Monsieur Casteret had told me that to be properly warm in a sleeping-bag one should wear almost no garments, and certainly not thick ones, so I was wearing nothing but pyjamas. It does not often happen to anyone to sleep in a cave in pyjamas! The sleeping-bag was very comfortable, and I did not find the ground too hard. It must be said that I am not in the habit of sleeping on soft mattresses.

My bed was on the left side of the small, low chamber, up against a wall adorned with very pretty little columns. At its head was the "flat" through which we had come, and beyond its foot the steep gully leading down to the chasm. To my right was the place where we had had our meal, so there were at least those few yards for me to move in if I needed to get up.

The silence was absolute—as Monsieur Casteret called it, "a mineral silence". It is not a silence like any other, but deeper and denser; yet not the silence of nothingness, but a silence filled with life, the life which here more than elsewhere is endlessly creating itself. I could now hear occasional drops of water at their millennial work. Except for this I could hear nothing, absolutely nothing— only the imaginary sound of distant, silvery bells.

I knew those tinkling bells. I had lain listening to them in bed at night when I was a child, before going to sleep. Monsieur Casteret told me that he, too, had often heard them in the mineral silence of the cave—a very pleasant illusion.

It was time to go to sleep. Our journey here had been tiring and thrilling, and I needed rest. I twisted and turned in my sleeping-bag, trying to find just the right position; but I could not get to sleep.

Finally I gave up and started to tell the beads of the rosary, not because I was afraid—on the contrary, I was very happy there—but because, like my companion a short time before, I thought my surroundings wonderful and very propitious to prayer. Beside, there was the incised Chrisma on the floor below. I was creating a link between the present day and the early centuries of the Christian era.

I was deeply stirred. I had wished for so long to know the world of caves. I had never doubted that one day I would visit it, without knowing when or how it would come about. But despite this I was a little astonished that it should really be happening to me. I felt very small and insignificant, a novice cave-explorer, and I thanked the Lord of all things for His understanding and love.

I heard something very strange, like the cry of a small child. Then silence again. Perhaps the sound had been produced by a drop of water falling into a hollow stalagmite. This sometimes happens underground.

The tiny incident did not alarm or astonish me. I mention it because when one is underground, if one is not to feel afraid, one must try at once to account for any sound one hears, before the imagination gets to work on it.

The time was a quarter to ten. I heard the tiny, shrill sound again, and this time I was sure it was not an hallucination. I went on listening. It seemed to happen at regular ten-minute intervals, which was logical if it was caused by a drop of water.

Ordinarily I do not take a watch with me into caves or up mountains. As I have already said, I like to lose all sense of time so as to be able to relax completely. But tonight, on Monsieur Casteret's advice, I was wearing my wristwatch.

That particular sound ceased, but I heard more drops of water and even the sound of a flake of calcite falling from the roof. Under that low ceiling every sound was magnified. When I shifted my position I made the strangest noises, and I could very clearly hear the beating of my heart.

Since I still could not sleep I decided to get up. After all, I had all night to sleep in. But what was I to do? I was sure that if I crawled into the "flat" I would make all kinds of interesting and exciting discoveries, but I could not break my promise not to leave that spot, so in the end I lay down again.

I sang the scouts' song . . .

Monsieur Casteret had said that people behaved in two ways when they were alone underground. Either they kept absolutely quiet so as not to set up echoes, or not to betray their presence; or else they talked and sang to keep themselves company. I had replied that I would be one of the first kind, but now here I was, singing. I also recited poems. There was no echo but a splendid resonance.

And still I could not sleep. Total silence. It is certainly true that, below ground, intimate converse with a Divine Presence is always possible . . .

I recited the names of every member of my family. They would never know how happy I was that night; but at least I could speak their names aloud underground and think of them. It was amusing to reflect that at that moment they must be asleep, never dreaming that I was alone in a cave. For that matter, they did not even know of the existence of this particular cave. What would they say when they heard about it? . . . But for the present the night was mine, and mine alone the happiness I felt. A selfish happiness, but such as we all need from time to time.

(Monsieur Casteret said afterwards: "Well, you were entitled to it. You aren't likely to have many competitors!")

Midnight. Again I heard that distant, near-human cry. (Monsieur Casteret said that it was probably a stone-marten.) I went on singing songs and anthems, and presently lit the acetylene lamp, which started at once, with the first match. I was rather proud of myself, although it was true that the carbide was probably still damp. I wriggled into a sitting position and with my head well down, to avoid stalactites, wrote on my pad.

Still the same uplifting and comforting silence. We need it so much in our civilisation; we have almost forgotten what silence is. I thought of Monsieur Casteret. Probably he was not getting much sleep either. He must be wondering what I was doing and looking forward to hearing what I had to tell him. He is the best, the simplest and the most extraordinary person I know. I draw sustenance from his counsel, for he is at the very heart of things. I owe him the greatest happiness I have ever known, and his friendship and his teaching are to me great and unmerited honours.

I also thought about Pierre Termier, the great French geologist and great Christian.

Although I was now sitting up I was not in the least cold. Nor was I afraid. I thought of my distant prehistoric ancestors, the Aurignacian and Magdalenian men who once lived on the lower storey of this cave and left their fingerprints behind. Like me, they lay down to rest on the hard ground, and what did they think about? About hunting and food, no doubt. And then there were children—how did they bring them up? We shall never know.

Giant cave-bears came into this place—Monsieur Casteret had referred jokingly to them. One could feel the imprint of their paws in the hardened clay. I should not have wanted to sleep here twenty thousand years ago. What would I do if one of those prehistoric monsters suddenly appeared before me out of the depths of time? Well—I would do nothing. Yet our forebears found ways of dealing with them. I admire them for it, and that is all I can say.

Plop! A drop of water fell tactlessly in my ear. But I had no right to complain, there were very few.

Half past twelve. I put out the lamp because I was feeling drowsy. My sleeping-bag was very warm.

Friday, 31st August, 1962. Four a.m.

I went on writing my diary. I had just woken up. I felt very rested and not too stiff, but I had a feeling that the damp was creeping into my bones. The silence was still the same, impenetrable, and again in the distance I seemed to hear the tinkling of tiny bells.

No drops of water at all were falling, and this was something worthy of note. I felt very much at home, even more relaxed than last night. I got up for a few minutes, but it was cold and I soon got back into my sleeping-bag.

There was a great assortment of odds and ends in the rucksack— a stalactite, a spare nozzle for the lamp, a press-button and—a piece of candle! I was very pleased. I resolved to light it, because I was in absolute darkness, not having made any kind of light since I woke up. Monsieur Casteret had said that he hadn't brought any candles—he had forgotten about this piece.

So, simply for pleasure and because it added a touch of local colour, I lit it. Well, it was not quite as easy as that. The wick must have been damp. It took several matches, but in the end I lit it and stuck it in the clay. While it was burning I went on writing inside my bag. The cave was beginning to feel really cold and damp.

So far as my small experience goes there is nothing alarming in a night spent underground. I shall do it again often if I can; it is a unique experience. Those hours of solitude—sacred, divine solitude!—seemed very short. No one before me had ever slept in that unknown part of the Gargas cave.

Lying on my back I wrote my initials, C.R., in blue on the ceiling above my head. I doubt very much if anyone will ever visit that place and read them.

The candle burned very slowly. Suddenly I thought I heard a distant, muffled sound, but then I decided that it was nothing; one sometimes hears creaks and rumblings underground that one cannot explain.

But then I heard it again, quite distinctly, a sound of footsteps. The time was exactly 4.48, and Monsieur Casteret was not supposed to come until six. Moreover he had said that he would whistle to warn me. Who could it be? I prayed that if it was some other person they would get lost in the "flat" and never reach me. I blew out the candle and stopped writing, because writing braille makes a slight noise . . .

And then I heard a whistle—three times! I answered it, and in a few minutes Monsieur Casteret arrived.

"You've robbed me of an hour of silence!" I said.

"How's that?"

"It's scarcely five."

We clasped hands, both very happy.

"I've had a wonderful night. I want to do it again. Last night I heard you for seven minutes while you were crawling through the 'flat', and this morning I heard you for ten minutes. How do you account for the difference?"

"Simply that it takes longer to get here because one's going uphill. I didn't know this cave was so resonant. But you must have heard me a long way off."

"Yes, I wondered who it was."

"There's a smell of snuffed-out candle in here."

"I found one in your rucksack and lit it, but I blew it out when I heard footsteps."

"You couldn't have been more alone. Gargas is very isolated."

"I know. Your grandson, Henri, told me that it's some miles from any inhabited place."

"My daughter, Gilberte, is waiting outside. She's impatient to hear all about how you spent the night. She would have come in with me, but she's still suffering from the effect of the bad fall she had in the mountains a month ago."

The temperature outside, even at that hour of the morning, seemed to me stifling after the chill of the cave. Gilberte was waiting by the car. The first question she asked was: "Did you think about the Ogre last night?"

"What ogre?"

"The Ogre of Gargas."

"What do you mean? Is it a joke?"

"No," said Monsieur Casteret seriously, "it's perfectly true. The Ogre of Gargas really did exist in the eighteenth century. His name was Blaise Ferrage, and he was the terror of the region. He carried off girls and grown women and devoured them in the cave. He tortured and ate thirty-two. The Government had to send troops to smoke him out and capture him. He was tried at Toulouse and condemned to be broken on the wheel. I didn't say anything about it yesterday because it was not a nice story to tell a girl who was going to spend the night alone in the cave."

"I'm thankful you didn't. I'm sure I should have found the thought disturbing. Well, at least I can congratulate myself on being the first woman to spend a night in the Gargas cave and come out alive!"

8

My First Chasm

To leave a cold and foggy Paris and be transported overnight to a place one loves is among the greatest pleasures in life. On 13th April, 1963, just before Easter, Monsieur Casteret and I were together again in the beautiful Forest of Gargas in the Hautes-Pyrenees (which I was inclined to think of as my own private domain) walking up a mountainside in the direction of the Puits de la Listre, also called the "Puits du General".

There were four other members of the party, Monsieur Casteret's daughter Raymonde and her husband Maxime Felix, Jacques Jolfre who had been with us in Riousec and Labastide the year before, and a youngster called Yves Barre; they had gone on ahead to fix the tackle for the chasm we were going to descend.

Monsieur Casteret and I talked our heads off while we rejoiced in the charm of the sun-bathed wood with its many scents. There were beech trees and box and a great variety of wild flowers, violets, cowslips, anemones, lungwort, clematis, hyacinths and different kinds of moss, damp with dew. It was like being in fairyland. We climbed slowly upward over a soft carpet smelling of dead leaves.

"Why has the Puits de la Listre got two names?" I asked.

"It's also called the Puits du General, the General's pit, because I descended it for the first time in 1936, with General Lafon and my friend Henri Casteran. The General might have been a young man from the way he behaved, although he was sixty-one. He had practised a great many kinds of sport, but this was new to him and he was delighted. The pit is over three hundred feet deep and absolutely vertical, as you'll see."

"How did you discover that it communicated with the Tignahustes cave?"

"I'd suspected it for a long time, because when I was bat-watching in Tignahustes I found a gap in the roof of the second chamber with an air current blowing through it which varied in strength according to the time of year. That was an indication, and it seemed to me that the draught could only come from the nearby Puits de la Listre. But it wasn't until January 1963 that we cleared a narrow bottleneck in the Tignahustes cave giving access to a shaft about a hundred feet deep which we explored two days later. I was the first to go down and I found myself in the great chaotic chamber of which the further part is at the bottom of the Puits de la Listre."

"How could you be sure of that? Caves look very much alike, particularly when they're full of boulders and debris."

"I found footprints preserved in the clay—the ones we had made in 1936."

"It must have been terribly exciting to find your own footprints!"

"Well, yes, but they were only twenty-seven years old. I've found footprints twenty-five thousand years old!"

"And you didn't climb out by way of the Puits de la Listre? What we're going to do today is something that has never been done before, isn't it? How wonderful!"

"Yes, this will be the first time anyone has done the round trip, from one shaft to the other. But we shall be going the opposite way, down the Listre and up through the Tignahustes, making a sort of vertical U-turn."

We walked on slowly, passing a *palombière*, a "hide" built in a tree, used by pigeon-shooters during the migratory season. I was very happy. I was going to realise one of my greatest ambitions, the descent of a real pot-hole by means of an "electron" ladder hanging in space. But I was quite calm, without any undue feeling of excitement or impatience. I had long awaited this moment and now it had come; I was living and enjoying it.

At the same time I had a sense of disappointment which I did my best to conceal. Monsieur Casteret would not be making the descent with me. A recent, very difficult underground expedition had left him too exhausted. He would help us from above, and then he and Yves, who was too young for the climb, would go round to the mouth of the Tignahustes cave to meet us when we emerged. It would be the first time I had been underground without him, and I deeply regretted it. But I should have three very experienced companions in Raymonde, Maxime and Jacques, and I was determined to do him credit.

We found when we reached the pit that the others had already secured and let down the ladder. Jacques was loading his camera for the colour photographs he meant to take down below, and Maxime and Raymonde were setting up the tackle for the safety-rope. We all put on climbing kit. As usual I wore canvas overalls, a helmet and thick boots.

I sat waiting on a moss and ivy-covered rock while Monsieur Casteret brought me flowers and plants to examine. Birds were singing, and I switched on my tape-recorder. We were going to make a sound-recording of the expedition. To carry that very fragile apparatus down into a chasm was no small undertaking, but it was worthwhile for the sake of a lasting record.

Jacques was the first to go down, and his voice came to us out of the depths, rising indignantly when, for a joke, we put a stop on the safety-rope. It echoed as though he were in a cathedral, which gave us some indication of the size of the shaft. Finally he signalled, by two blasts of his whistle, that he had arrived at the first stage.

The safety-rope was hauled up and Raymonde went down to join him. The first stage, at a depth of about a hundred and twenty feet, was a narrow, sloping shelf.

It was now my turn and I left my moss-covered rock. I was quite calm but a little apprehensive when it came to taking the plunge. Monsieur Casteret checked my safety-belt, and deciding that it did not fit well enough gave me another, to which he made the rope fast. Then to give me confidence he made me feel the rope and tackle, which would take my weight if I let go of the ladder, and the ladder itself and the means used to ensure that it was properly secured.

Maxime spoke words of encouragement in his quiet, lilting voice, and I lowered myself over the edge and set my foot on the first rung of the ladder. I now wanted to get on fast to where the ladder was hanging free, because at the top it was tight against the rim of the pit so that I pinched my fingers and could not find the rungs with my feet. This was a difficult moment. "I'm going to let go!" I thought—and below me was a three-hundred-foot drop! I forgot about the safety-rope, but it was still there, and so was Monsieur Casteret, talking to me from above.

"Don't be so tense, and don't hang on your arms. Try to get down fast because it's less tiring. You'll soon get used to it."

"No, I shan't!"

"You'll have to," he replied.

I could hear Jacques and Raymonde below me talking as they followed my descent. They could see the ladder jerking and they could see me, a black shape against the bright mouth of the pit. Dead leaves were whirling round me, and I must have loosened stones in passing because I heard Jacques exclaim to Raymonde, "Watch out!"

I called down to Jacques: "I'm swinging!"

"Never mind. Just carry on."

"It's rather alarming."

I did not say much, preferring to save my breath. I tried to go down quickly and nimbly, as Monsieur Casteret had advised, but I was too frightened. The ladder was spinning, the shaft was widening, and the whistle of falling stones gave me a horrible feeling, the sort of moral vertigo I had known in the mountains.

"Don't grip the ladder too tight," said Jacques with a chuckle. "You know how brittle they are."

"Oh, now you're terrifying me!"

I could hear Raymonde laughing.

I went on down. Monsieur Casteret was leaning over the edge to speak to me, and I could imagine his head silhouetted against the sky. He assured me that everything was all right. I was scarcely talking at all, and to make me say something Maxime slowed up the unwinding of the safety-rope. My reaction was instantaneous.

"Keep that rope slack, will you!"

Monsieur Casteret was now talking to Jacques and Raymonde, asking if they had a line ready to pull in the ladder. It was nice to know that preparations were being made for my arrival. I was now about halfway down the first stage, and I could hear stones falling past me and drops of water, which were somehow comforting. I was getting used to the flexibility of the ladder and the clicking of its rungs. For the second time I called for more slack in the rope. The shaft seemed to me perfectly cylindrical, and it was remarkably resonant.

"Colette," called Monsieur Casteret. "Do keep talking. Don't forget the tape-recorder's running."

"I'm too out of breath."

At that moment I was struggling to control the ladder with my back against the wall—there must have been a bulge. I tried to turn it so as to face the wall, but all I did was to start it swinging, and knobs of stalagmite bruised my back. I had not yet mastered the technique, which is to keep the knees well apart so that the ladder is close to one's body.

"You're doing fine," said Jacques. "Only a few more yards. I expect you'll come out alive—and at Tignahustes!"

"Tignahustes seems a very long way off. I'm exhausted."

"Well, rest for a little while, Colette," said Raymonde, "with your back against the wall."

I should have liked to, but I was afraid that if I leaned back against the wall the ladder would swing out into space and I would lose my grip. I preferred to go on and get it over, since there was only a short way to go. To ease the strain on my hands I crossed my arms in front of me grasping the ladder from behind. The last fifteen rungs called for a great effort. That ladder was like a bit of spider's web, about six inches wide, just enough to put a foot on, and its steel-cable side-members were extremely thin and horribly slippery. Jacques took a photograph of me in action.

"I can't find the next rung!" I said.

"It's a bit to the right of your foot. Now keep still and we'll pull you in to the shelf. That's it. Now you can step on to the rock."

I let go the ladder and clasped Jacques' hand.

"Happy landing!" we shouted for the benefit of those above.

"Splendid!" came Monsieur Casteret's voice. "Do you want to go on, or would you rather come back?"

"I'm going on."

"Good girl!"

I unhitched the safety-rope and we blew two blasts of the whistle as a signal for it to be hauled up for Maxime.

While we waited for him to join us Raymonde gave me a bat which she had picked off the wall, plunged in its winter sleep. I have a particular fondness for bats, having learnt so much about them from Monsieur Casteret in the Tignahustes cave. I felt that this was my reward for my first descent into a real abyss and that it would bring me luck. I clasped it in my hand, but gently, because it was very fragile—like happiness.

Monsieur Casteret was bombarding us with bits of moss, partly
as a joke but also from a cave-explorer's impulse to measure the
depth of any pit. But a piece got lodged in the rungs of the ladder
and we asked him not to. Then I threw a stone to get an idea of the
depth below us and this, too, called forth a rebuke, because it might
damage the ladder.

Maxime joined us on the shelf and asked me how I had got on.

"I found this first part rather difficult." I said. "I kept banging
my back against the wall, and then the ladder swung out into
space. I seemed to be hanging on by my toes and fingertips."

"But that always happens. The ladder always tends to swing
away from the wall. You have to learn to control it, and you should
always keep your hands at the level of your face. You'll find the
next stage easier. It's only about seventy feet."

Jacques started on the second stage, which took him down to a
depth of nearly two hundred feet. Then it was my turn. Helped by
Raymonde and Maxime I moved to the edge of the shelf and
gripped the ladder. There was again that moment of panic, that
crucial moment when one leaves terra firma to trust oneself to a
swinging ladder that seems impossibly small and frail. But then,
when this was over, I had a sudden feeling of rapture.

Yes, of rapture! I wasn't frightened this time. Maxime had
explained the technique and I knew that I was well roped. The
shaft was wider. For the first time I knew the joy of a free descent,
clear of the walls. Monsieur Casteret had told me that a descent
by ladder could be very pleasant, and now I knew what he meant.
It was almost like flying. I went down without any trouble, calling
to Jacques that I was on my way.

"I'm ready for you," said Jacques. "You're nearly here. Stop
for a moment while I take a photograph. Fine! Now I'll pull
you in."

This second stage was a large recess with an overhang in the
wall of the shaft. It was very pretty with stalagmite decorations
and draperies. I sat down to rest on a lump of stalagmite and while
talking to Jacques examined the contents of my pockets—an indelible pencil, a small penknife and a pebble I had picked up at
our first stopping place to add to my collection.

The ladder began to shake as the next person came down, and
presently the four of us were together again, talking excitedly in

that solitary, unknown place. We brushed pebbles into the abyss to clear the floor, and then Raymonde and Jacques unrolled the ladder for the last stage of the descent, which would take us to a depth of three hundred feet.

Maxime shouted up to Monsieur Casteret, whose voice now reached us very faintly, to ask the time. We hadn't a watch between us. We had started the descent at half past two, and it was now nearly four.

"It's raining," I said to the others.

"So it is! We should have brought umbrellas."

In fact there was a considerable seepage of water, which is why there were so many stalagmite formations.

Raymonde was the first to embark on the final stage. She seemed to enjoy it, because we could hear her whistling and singing. I asked her if the ladder was hanging clear or if it was against the wall, but her reply was vague. However, I didn't mind, I would find out for myself and it would be a piece of real exploration. I called up to tell Monsieur Casteret when she reached the bottom.

"And now it's my turn!"

"What?"

"It's my turn."

"Well, keep your head, and good luck."

Maxime roped me when Raymonde sent back the safety-rope, and the two men drew the swinging ladder towards me and helped me on to it while we all talked at once, questions, answers and words of advice flying back and forth. Then I started on the last downward climb and Jacques took another photograph. He had advised me to use my hands as little as possible, simply brushing them over the rungs. I went down quickly, but presently found myself in a narrow bottleneck where I bumped against the rocks; I had to keep the ladder close to my body.

I had not much to say while I was negotiating this chimney, a fact which drew from the other members of the party a comment to the effect that no news was presumably good news. The truth was that my overalls had got caught on a projecting piece of rock, and I was performing all sorts of acrobatics in my efforts to free it. "Keep calm," I said to myself. "There is always a way of solving these problems." The ladder was whipping about, being rendered particularly lively by the length of the drop. I hung on to a rung with my right hand while I tried to release myself with my left. The others called to me but I was too busy to answer. Although the delay was very short it seemed to go on for ever, and I caught myself muttering unintelligible words which may have been prayers but sounded more like the language of the original cave-dwellers.

At last I managed it. Down below Raymonde was singing. The hundred feet of that last stage seemed very long, but I was pleased with myself for having been equal to the emergency. My love of exploring was restored, and I knew that I should descend many more chasms.

I reported my arrival with the agreed signal of four blasts on the whistle, and then set about examining my immediate surroundings, which were largely clay. I found another bat hanging upside down waiting for the Spring. The two men joined Raymonde and me. Now we were all at the bottom of the Puits de la Listre, three hundred feet below ground. I wrote my initials and the date on a rock, thinking as I did so of Monsieur Casteret's visit to this spot with General Lafon, twenty-seven years earlier. I wished we did not have to tread out their footprints, but it was unavoidable.

There was a lot of water dripping in this dank and chilly spot, where the ground was covered with the bones of animals—sheep, dogs and martens—dashed to death after a terrible fall.

We picked our way through a chaos of boulders and rubble, climbing over rocks, wriggling under them, climbing up small chimneys. While we were doing so I groped about for fragments to keep as souvenirs. My overall was so caked with clay that I could not undo the zip-fastener of the pocket to get at my handkerchief.

Finally we reached the bottom of the Tignahustes shaft, at the top of which Monsieur Casteret and Yves were awaiting us, having gone there above ground. They had already let down the ladder, and attached to it we found a note from Monsieur Casteret which read, "Lift out of order. Visitors are requested to use the service stairs."

This shaft was about a hundred and thirty feet, with a stage some thirty feet from the bottom; but it was very much narrower than the Listre pit. Jacques climbed up to the stage and I followed him. The ladder was extremely slippery. I got my fingers pinched and debris showered down, forcing Raymonde to duck her head.

Maxime was the first to reach the surface, then Jacques. Then the safety-rope was sent down again and it was my turn to climb up to daylight—or rather, to the light of my friends' lanterns, for I should be surfacing in the Tignahustes Cave, in the tunnel that had been cleared that winter.

I roped myself, not feeling sorry to leave that damp and chilly place, where for some little time I had been crouched on a narrow ledge. I shouted to the party above, "This ladder's disgusting!" and Jacques replied, "Would you like me to come down and wipe it for you?"

I started to climb. A lively conversation was going on above. I could not make out what was being said, but I imagine Monsieur Casteret was asking how I had got on during that underground journey from one cave to the other.

"I'm going to rest for a moment," I called.

"All right, but don't put too much weight on your arms."

I enjoyed that climb. I enjoyed touching the rock and feeling the strange patterns caused by erosion. There are celebrated junctions betwen caves—that between the Marcel Loubens and the Henne-Morte, for instance, and the one between the Trou du Vent and the Gouffre Pierre. The one we had pioneered today was quite modest, but it was rare to have the chance of establishing a junction of any kind, and this thought gave me intense pleasure.

"I'm starting again."

"Right!"

I came to a very narrow part of the shaft and banged my head; it was a good thing I had a helmet. Jacques called down that it had come in sight, although this was not true; he was simply saying it to encourage me.

There were shouts of, "Heaven helps those who help themselves," and, "Watch your head!"

"I can't get through!" I said.

"But you can. You've done it!"

Helped by my friends I got to my feet in the narrow tunnel, to be greeted by Monsieur Casteret.

"Well, did you have a good trip?"

"Wonderful," I said breathlessly.

"Which part did you find most difficult?"

"The first stage of the descent."

I told Monsieur Casteret about my feelings and discoveries.

"Right at the bottom there are little hollows full of water, and there were musical stalagmite draperies, but they were too high up for me to be able to make them ring . . . Of course the best moment was arriving there, three hundred feet down; but what I liked most of all was the descent of the second stage, and that big, overhanging chamber . . . To me it was all so wonderfully new. I feel I want to explore lots of other pits and chasms. I'm not nearly as tired as I expected to be."

"It was thrilling for me too," said Monsieur Casteret, "even though I couldn't go with you. I could hear the sound of your movements and remember how I went down there with the General and Henri Casteran. So now you've gone down the Listre and come up in a cave you already know, the Tignahustes!"

And that is cave-exploring!

Epilogue

I HAVE come to the end of this small testimony to the splendour of mountains and caves, and I am grateful to those readers who have accompanied me so far. If they have found in my story something of their own youth and youthful dreams I shall have fulfilled my purpose.

But there are readers who may still ask, how can a blind girl be so in love with Nature? Why does she write about it as though she can see? And they may be amazed and even dismayed to discover that she can be as thrilled as any other person in the pursuit of very strenuous and dangerous pastimes.

To these I can only answer that the blind like to behave like other people and try to "grope" as little as possible. And at the risk of repeating myself I will add that there is less difference than one may think between the "world of the blind" and the world that sees. I hope that this book, in one or other of its chapters, will contain something of encouragement for every reader, so that in the worst moments of sadness and solitude he will find in it something to sustain him.

In the twentieth century, when science is making such giant strides in every field, pity and indulgence for the blind are no longer appropriate. What we want is more understanding and less foolish prejudice. Given the will, even those who cannot see can do difficult things; and I hope that my message will be of some help in causing this to be realised.

Let your heart be uplifted by the almost Divine magic of peaks and underground landscapes and do not be afraid to dream. Perhaps one day handicapped children in the schools of France and other countries will sit dreaming over their manuals of geography and geology . . . For my part, I have given the best of myself, the freshness of my youth and the ardour and aspirations of my soul, to this captivating and mysterious adventure.

In conclusion may I be allowed one final reminiscence. I am thinking of the moving and solemn moment when the Abbé Dunoyer, almoner of the Monastère des Myriams, returned my ice-axe to me after blessing it.

"May this ice-axe save you from the traps and snares of the mountains. In blessing it I bless the mountains, and in blessing the mountains let us think of all those who have died in them."

But the mountains are life itself; and for all of us there are many other dreams in life requiring to be fulfilled, to be made known and made loved. With my inward gaze fixed on the mountains I was in danger of missing the miracle at the side of the path. There are many miracles, whether we recognise them or refuse to see them, but there is only one path, that of Life; the life which goes on, which rises causing us to rise, which breaks out everywhere, and in which we must play our part with all the strength we possess for the greater good of Creation.

After climbing Alpine peaks I had the inexpressible delight of exploring Pyrenean caves. That scientific rapture is something that many humans will never know, for no solitude, no darkness, can compare with those of the subterranean world.

I sat alone for half an hour on the summit of the Col Infranchissable, it is true; but I passed a whole night alone in an unexplored level of the Gargas cave.

Up in the heights the silence is white and luminous, a poetry of sunshine, glaciers, keen air and the scent of snow—the harmony of the whole being. Underground it is a mineral stillness, immovable, a mysteriously living silence of dropping water and the smell of clay. It is both joy and anguish, every sense alert, the mind registering the slightest sound, the smallest detail. There are strange creakings to be heard, unexplicable cries which puzzle the speleologist.

Human traces in the snow are effaced in a few hours; in the caves they may survive for twenty thousand years.

The marvellous contrasts in Nature—how can any youthful, ardent spirit fail to respond to their appeal?

All the mountains in France are known, but there are still potholes and caverns to be discovered and explored—how can we not dream of them?

To discover, to learn, to believe in one's luck, to compel Destiny and never doubt that great achievements are possible, even though they go far beyond our small conceptions; to believe in Divine strength and human worth, to thirst for still more knowledge . . .

That is the well-spring and the grand secret of life.